My Father

Praise for the Book

'Illuminating and deeply moving, Arvind Panagariya's *My Father* traces the progress and upheaval of twentieth-century India through the life of one dedicated civil servant – as Panagariya puts it, an ordinary man living an extraordinary life. Baloo Lal Panagariya's story, deftly told by his son, is a fascinating tale that spans the personal and the political. An eye-opening read.'

– **Shashi Tharoor**, member of Parliament and author

'Arguably the most influential economist on the Indian policy scene today, Arvind Panagariya reveals an astonishing talent for storytelling in this moving portrayal of his grandmother and father. In their grit and determination, which led the family from penury to prosperity, lies an inspirational tale of social mobility available to anyone willing to work for it.'

– **Padma Desai**, Professor Emerita of Economics, Columbia University, and author

'A simple, charming, old-fashioned tale of a decent man who struggles to rise from poverty into the middle class, from a pre-modern life to a modern life. Such a person's life, honestly captured, is not only unique but the only certain data of history we possess.'

– **Gurcharan Das**, author

'Arvind Panagariya tells the riveting story of his father who was born in abject poverty in a village, lost his father at five and mother at fourteen, and yet rose up to help build his state. In parallel, he offers a fascinating account of life in the pre- and post-independence Rajasthan and what the freedom movement meant in the nation's princely states.'

– **N.K. Singh**, chairman, Fifteenth Finance Commission, and author

'Truly a masterpiece! The narrative, with India's evolving history as background, makes for extremely compelling reading. Outside of, maybe, Nirad Chaudhary's *Autobiography of an Unknown Indian*, I haven't read any such personalized story interwoven with the history of India.'

– **Pravin Krishna**, Chung Ju Yung Distinguished Professor of Economics and Business, Johns Hopkins University

My Father

the extraordinary life of an ordinary man

Arvind Panagariya

HarperCollins *Publishers* India

First published in India by
HarperCollins *Publishers* in 2021
A-75, Sector 57, Noida, Uttar Pradesh 201301, India
www.harpercollins.co.in

2 4 6 8 10 9 7 5 3 1

Photos courtesy of the author

P-ISBN: 978-93-5422-285-6
E-ISBN: 978-93-5422-293-1

Typeset in 12/16 Adobe Garamond at
Manipal Technologies Limited, Manipal

Printed and bound at
Thomson Press (India) Ltd.

MIX
Paper
FSC FSC™ C010615

This book is produced from independently certified FSC™ paper
to ensure responsible forest management.

To
Dhapubai

The grand grandmother who made it all possible for us

Contents

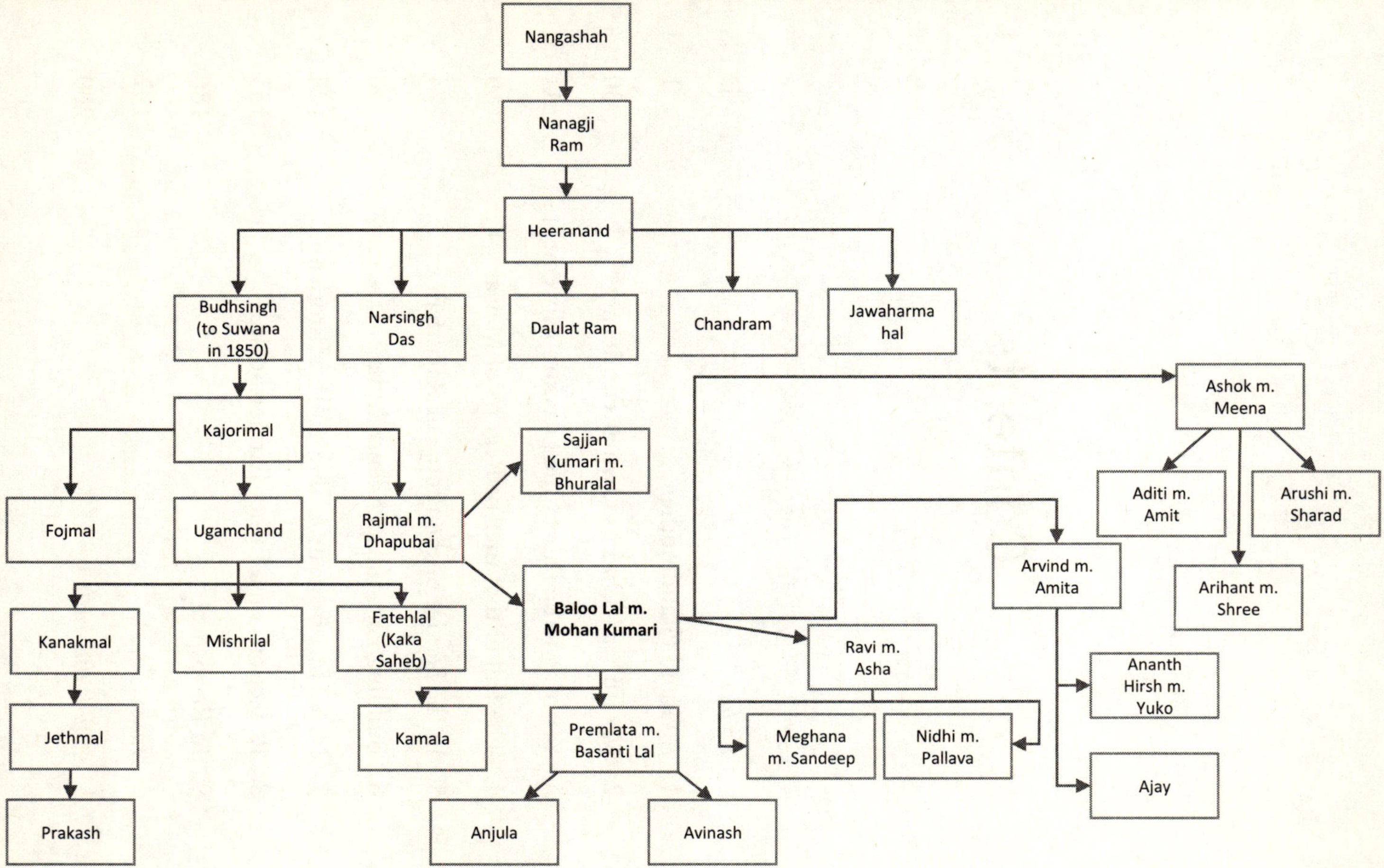
Nangashah
Nanagji Ram
Heeranand
Budhsingh (to Suwana in 1850)
Narsingh Das
Daulat Ram
Chandram
Jawaharmahal
Kajorimal
Fojmal
Ugamchand
Rajmal m. Dhapubai
Sajjan Kumari m. Bhuralal
Baloo Lal m. Mohan Kumari
Kanakmal
Mishrilal
Fatehlal (Kaka Saheb)
Jethmal
Prakash
Kamala
Premlata m. Basanti Lal
Anjula
Avinash
Ravi m. Asha
Meghana m. Sandeep
Nidhi m. Pallava
Arvind m. Amita
Ananth Hirsh m. Yuko
Ajay
Ashok m. Meena
Aditi m. Amit
Arihant m. Shree
Arushi m. Sharad

Preface

AS THE TITLE OF the book makes amply clear, this is a biography of my father, Baloo Lal Panagariya. The question many readers would ask is why they should be interested in it. I can imagine that at least some readers would have an interest in my autobiography, or a memoir by me covering the period of my close association with Prime Minister Narendra Modi. But what could possibly be the case for a biography of my father, who retired as a deputy secretary in the Government of Rajasthan in 1976 and was barely known outside his own state? I believe I owe the reader an answer to this question at the outset.

First and foremost, the generation born during the 1920s, to which my father belonged, was a special one. It straddled pre- and post-Independence India in a way like no other. It was too young to be at the forefront of the freedom movement, and yet old enough to be inspired by its foremost leader, Mahatma

Gandhi, and to join him in his endeavours. Importantly, it was also a generation that came of age just as India was becoming independent and was thus positioned just right to help build the country post Independence. Born in 1921, my father was twenty-six years old at the time of Independence. Therefore, he witnessed Mahatma Gandhi lead India to independence from the British during the formative years of his life and still had many years ahead of him to help build a new nation. Did he rise to the occasion? I will explore this in my book.

India is a vast country; a few well-known national political figures and handful of distinguished members of the civil service in the central government alone could not have built it. Ultimately, the country was the sum of its constituent states, and each state had to be shaped and built. What role did ordinary citizens like my father play in building their states? In many states, the local political leadership was not fully equipped to govern them. At the same time, the number of officers helping run the state governments was small. Those facts empowered even junior officers to exert influence on outcomes. If they were able and motivated to promote the public interest, as my father was, they could influence outcomes in ways that could contribute to the welfare of many generations to come.

The lives of ordinary citizens can also provide a window to the social, cultural and political ethos of their times. What was life like for ordinary citizens in rural India of the 1920s and 1930s? What opportunities existed for them? How did they relate to the national movement, in which Mahatma Gandhi had tried to involve every Indian in one way or the other?

Answers to these questions become particularly interesting when probed through the life of someone who came from a state like Rajasthan, as Rajasthan was formed by merging a large number of independent princely states that local hereditary kings, rather than the British government, ruled. The British government had maintained control over these states through an agent of the governor general, but left their day-to-day administration to the local kings.

The cause of misery of the people in the princely states was often poor governance and exploitation by the local kings. But both Mahatma Gandhi and the Indian National Congress were reluctant to turn the freedom movement into a movement against the local kings. As such, until as late as 1938, they had an explicit policy of limiting the freedom movement to the eleven provinces that the British ruled directly. This fact made it difficult for young men like my father, who grew up in a princely state, to participate actively in the freedom movement. Even in 1938, when the Congress changed its policy, it forbade local movements in the princely states from using its name. Instead, it encouraged each state to form its own Praja Mandal (public association) under whose auspices it could conduct its movement against local misrule.

Apart from these considerations, my father's life would likely interest and, indeed, inspire many young readers, simply because of its unique trajectory. He was born in a remote village in Rajasthan, in a family so poor that it could not scrape together two square meals a day. The village did not have even a primary school until after he was twenty-one years old. He lost his father at the age of five. At fourteen, he lost his mother. What are the odds that a young man with this history would manage to land up in Jaipur at twenty-five years to serve on the editorial board of *Lokvani*, the only newspaper in the city, so that he could fulfil his desire to contribute to the freedom movement as it approached its logical conclusion? And who could have predicted that two of his sons would become so successful that the President of India would honour them with Padma awards, one with the Padma Shri and the other with the Padma Bhushan? Yet, that in a nutshell is my father's story.

I confess that I began this work as my own autobiography. I had known of the extreme hardships my father had faced during his early life from a short autobiography that he had written for circulation among family members. My plan was to include this family background in my autobiography. Therefore, I began with a chapter on my grandmother, whom I had never seen but who had greatly fascinated me from the bit I read about her in Father's autobiography. After completing the chapter on her, I began the second chapter, which was on my father. I had expected to summarize a few key facts of his life in twenty or twenty-five pages and then turn to my own. But as I progressed, this second chapter kept getting longer and longer, until I realized that the document was turning into my father's biography. At that point, I also realized that the story of my father's life was infinitely more interesting than mine. The result of that realization is this volume in the reader's hands.

Much of the source material for this biography comes from my father's unpublished autobiography. Having retired at the relatively young age of fifty-five, he had revived his interest in writing from the time he had helped edit *Lokvani* in Jaipur. He wrote several books, among which was the definitive work on the freedom movement in Rajasthan titled *Rajasthan Main Swatantrata Sangram* (The Freedom Movement in Rajasthan). The autobiography was among the last two books that remained unpublished. Instead, Father got his sister's son, who owned a printing press, to print one hundred copies of the autobiography and shared them with the extended family. Therefore, while this biography has my words, the story is as told by my father.

Writing this volume has been a family enterprise. Apart from the members of my immediate family, wife Amita and sons Ananth Hirsh and Ajay, my brothers, Ravi and Ashok, have contributed to it, directly or indirectly. Ravi read the entire manuscript and helped make several factual corrections. My bhabhi, Ashok's wife, Meena, enthusiastically collected many of the photographs. My friend Pravin Krishna, professor of international economics and business at Johns Hopkins University, read the penultimate draft in its entirety and provided some extremely useful suggestions. Given that this is the first time I have undertaken a project of this nature, his encouragement at a critical time proved extremely valuable. Petal Dhillon of the Ministry of Railways in the Government of India and Rajeev Mantri, managing director, Navam Capital also read an earlier version of the manuscript and provided extremely helpful comments. For the final extensive edits to the manuscript, I am deeply indebted to Kripa Raman and Amrita Mukerji, my editors at HarperCollins. However, none of those who have helped in the writing of this book is to be blamed for any indiscretions or errors in it, which remain solely my personal responsibility.

1

A Grand Grandmother

IF A HIGHER POWER were to grant me the wish to spend a few hours with a person of my choosing from amongst the living and dead, without a shred of doubt that person would be my paternal grandmother. Dhapubai, as she was known, lived no more than thirty-five years. She was long gone before any of my siblings or I was born. The family has no photograph, painting or sketch of her – they were simply too poor to afford such a luxury during her lifetime. But going by the few facts that I gathered from the short autobiography my father wrote, she must have been an amazing woman. I can say without hesitation that she is the fountainhead of all the good things that eventually happened to my father, mother, their children and their children's children. No doubt, my father's perseverance, diligence and foresight were critical to the good lives we, his children, could have, but none of that would have been possible had Dhapubai not made the supreme sacrifice of her life to nurture and educate him, against all odds, during the first fourteen years of his life.

Before I tell that story, however, let me describe in brief some early history of the family. It is necessary to go into this to give the reader a sense of how humble the origins of the family are and how ordinary its status had been throughout its known history. The only modest prosperity that the family experienced – and that too, only by the prevailing standards of those times in rural India – was during the lives of my father's great-grandfather and grandfather. By the time my father was born, its fortunes had sunk deep once again to the point of abject poverty. My father had had to rebuild life from scratch, aided only by his elementary-school education, for which his mother could pave the way, literally at the cost of her own life.

We belong to the Oswal community, whose origin traces back to the fifth century BCE in the small town of Osian near Jodhpur, in the Marwar region of Rajasthan. Legend has it that Jain Acharya Ratna Prabha Suri came to Osian in 457 BCE and successfully persuaded its king and people to give up meat and alcohol and embrace Jainism. These converts came to be known as Oswals. Starting some time in the tenth century CE, many of the Oswal families migrated to Sindh and to various parts of Rajasthan and Gujarat. If legend is to be believed, my ancestors came from one of these families.

According to the story passed on to my father by his elders, who in turn had got it from their elders, our ancestors first migrated to Panagarh, a village to the east of Osian in Nagaur district of Rajasthan. Unfortunately, the truth of this story cannot be verified. A source of some scepticism is that though a village by the name of Panagarh exists near Chittor in the Mewar region, no such village can be found on any of the maps in the entire Marwar region, let alone Nagaur district.

Be that as it may, sometime in the sixteenth century, my ancestors are said to have left drought-prone Panagarh and moved further east and south, into Mewar. They first went to Taswaria, then to Sindri, on to Sanganer, and finally settled in Suwana. All four of these villages are in Bhilwara district of Rajasthan. The last three are within a three-to-four-mile radius of the town of Bhilwara. All four villages exist today and can be found on maps readily available on the Internet. All appear on the rosters of the 2011 Census of India as well.

Once out of Panagarh, the family came to be known as Panagariya. Nangashah, the first ancestor known by name, initially lived in Sindri. All we know about him is that he was a devotee of Balaji (Hanuman) of Sindri, whose idol, in the form of a simple rock, stood on a raised but open platform made of solid stone until about forty years ago. Subsequently, the platform has been converted into a full-fledged temple, with four walls around the idol and a dome at the top. Even the idol has been given a makeover and now looks like a traditional idol of Hanuman. Nangashah's devotion to Balaji has been passed on from generation to generation and remains intact among nearly all family members up to the present day. It may have been greatly strengthened by an episode relating to the birth and survival of my father, which I will narrate later.

Sometime in the second half of the eighteenth century, Nangashah migrated from Sindri to Sanganer, a town founded by the legendary warrior Rana Sanga in the sixteenth century. Nangashah had one son, but all we know about him is his name and that he died in 1810 CE, leaving behind one male child. The child, named Heeranand, had five male children, of whom two died before reaching adulthood. A family document suggests that Heeranand lived a life of poverty.

Heeranand died in 1850, after which two of his sons migrated to Suwana in search of a better life. Their families and mother accompanied them. One of these two sons was Budhsingh, my father's great-grandfather. The third son remained in Sanganer, but his branch of the family ended with his great-grandson.

The great-grandson was a contemporary of my father's, and I remember visiting his place in Sanganer with the family during my childhood. There is at least one other Panagariya family in Sanganer that did not descend from Nangashah. Three male children from this family are my contemporaries; two of them are now settled in Bhilwara and the third in Jaipur.

Suwana, where Budhsingh, his brother and their families arrived around 1850, is located approximately three miles east of Bhilwara, a major town that serves as the headquarters of the district of the same name. Being located on the banks of the River Kothari, the village had a high water table, at least until the late 1950s, which allowed the residents to reap two crops a year. But after the construction of the Meja dam in 1958, the river dried up. Since then, only the fields falling in the command area of the Meja dam are able to produce two crops a year.

Agriculture was the mainstay of the bulk of the population. The farmers here, especially from the Jat community, which is dominant in the village, were sturdy people and were prosperous. During the 1920s and 1930s, when my father was growing up, the village had a population of approximately 3,000. It did not have a school, however, until as late as 1942. That year, the Mewar government opened the first primary school, with a single teacher.

There was a well in the heart of the village. Residents took water out of it and carried it home in pitchers on their heads for their daily use. On the outskirts of the village, there was a good-sized pond where people had their baths and also brought their livestock for a drink of water. This pond almost never dried up. I remember passing by both the well and the pond on my numerous visits to the village during my childhood. In the old days, there also existed a giant banyan tree on the banks of the pond. Legend has it that it was more than 500 years old. Hundreds of traders, with their bullock carts hauling goods for transport between Bijolia and Bhilwara, broke their journey here to rest under the shade of the tree and escape the heat, especially during the early part of the afternoon when the sun was intense. Sadly, the tree fell prey to old age several decades ago and exists no more.

A short distance from the well stands the temple of Charbhuja, dedicated to Lord Vishnu. According to a stone inscription in the temple, the village had existed as early as the tenth century CE. During my father's childhood, there was a place called 'garh', meaning 'fort', in the heart of the village. Having seen its ruins, he was convinced that it did exist at one time, although no fort stood there even at the time of my father's birth. According to a story floating around during his childhood, there was a big treasure hidden under the debris of the fort. As a result, many adventurous people had dug up the place but found nothing. During the last seven or eight decades, several houses have come up on the land, and the memory of the 'garh' having been there has been entirely wiped out.

According to the Census 2011, Suwana has 977 houses, a population of 5,158 and a literacy rate of 72 per cent.[1] During

---

1 Suwana Population, Census 2011, https://tinyurl.com/ttwc823n

my father's childhood, the vast majority of dwellings were kuchcha houses (fragile dwellings made of mud, wood and straw). But today, such houses are rare, with nearly all those dwellings having been replaced by pucca houses (houses made of sturdier materials, such as brick and cement). Internal pathways used to be mud roads even during my childhood. Pucca roads have come to replace them in recent years.

Budhsingh did well upon coming to Suwana. For the first time in its known history, the family experienced some measure of prosperity. According to family documents, Budhsingh engaged in the lucrative trade of opium and in the banking business, apart from agriculture. By 1870, he had accumulated enough wealth to construct a well-planned three-storeyed pucca house straight across from the Charbhuja temple.

This is a spacious house. The rooms on the ground floor served as storage space for opium, raw cotton and other commodities. There was an open yard in the middle, with an underground storage space for food grain, for emergencies such as drought. The family lived on the first floor, while the top floor was reserved for special guests, including newly-weds. The house is so strongly built that it has required no major repairs during its 150 years of existence. During many summer vacations, my mother would visit this family house, inevitably dragging us, the reluctant city children, with her.

The house is located centrally in the village. Two of the main pathways of the village meet directly outside the house in an L-shaped intersection. As you come out, there is a row of houses on the left, with the first house making a perpendicular with ours. As you cross the road and walk straight ahead, there are houses on both sides and the pathway leads you to the outer periphery of the village. Alternatively, if you turn right after coming out of the house and continue to walk, you pass the Charbhuja temple on your right and, after a short walk, arrive at the main well, where I would witness village residents drawing water and taking it home during my childhood. Our house and the Charbhuja temple are separated by another pathway, which makes a T-intersection with the one leading to the well. Therefore, ours is a corner house, and its windows on multiple sides allow ample flow of light as well as air.

As Budhsingh acquired wealth, he also gained in influence. He came to preside over the traditional panchayat (local self-government), which met from time to time on the grand platform of solid stone outside the house to settle all types of disputes among the villagers. Within the rural context, he had a highly successful and prosperous life.

Budhsingh died at a ripe old age in 1883. My father learned from village elders that drummers led his funeral procession, which was joined by his relatives, as well as friends and admirers from Suwana, numerous neighbouring villages and the nearby town of Bhilwara. Throughout the six-kilometre route to the banks of the Kothari, where the cremation took place, family members and relatives showered silver and copper coins along the path to honour him. His widow, who must have also been of advanced age, followed Budhsingh within a few days of his demise.

Following the death of Budhsingh, his only son Kajorimal took charge of the family. His very first act was to organize a grand community feast to commemorate the deaths of his parents, as per the tradition. The feast was spread over three days to accommodate thousands of invitees from as many as fifty-two localities in the nearby towns and villages. After observing all the ceremonies associated with the deaths, which lasted about a month, Kajorimal got down to resuming the family business.

Thanks to the wealth and the established businesses that he inherited, Kajorimal lived well for most of his life. He had two sons from his first wife, who came from a well-known family in Mewar. After her death, he married a second time. She was also from a distinguished family, and he had his third son, Rajmal, by her. The latter would be my grandfather and the future husband of Dhapubai. Born in 1900, Rajmal was several years younger than his oldest (step) brother. In due course, Kajorimal got his three sons married with great fanfare. His own two marriages and the marriages of the three sons connected the family to a number of prominent Oswal families of Mewar.

Kajorimal had given his second son in adoption to another family that had no male child. Therefore, only his oldest and youngest sons remained with him. The oldest son, Ugamchand, was an able young man who became his right-hand man in business. Rajmal was still a child at the time. With the father and the older son working together, the family continued to do well on the back of the lucrative opium trade.

Unfortunately, however, Ugamchand died young, in 1913. He left behind three sons. The oldest son, Kanakmal, was born in the same year as his uncle Rajmal and was thirteen years old at the time of Ugamchand's death; the other two sons were nine and two. The death of Ugamchand would be the first of a series of blows that would leave the family in tatters in a matter of just four years. My father would thus be born amid extreme poverty.

In 1858, control of all of India had passed on to the British government from the East India Company. For administrative purposes, the British had divided the country into two parts: a set of provinces they administered directly, and some 560-plus princely states, zamindaris and jagirdaris, which they let the local hereditary rulers govern. The latter were in a subsidiary relationship with the British Crown and were effectively its vassals. The hereditary rulers were obliged to take direction from and work under the overall supervision of a British agent.

Independent India created the current state of Rajasthan by merging nineteen princely states, two zamindaris and one directly ruled territory known as Ajmer-Merwara. A British agent governed Ajmer-Merwara under the overall supervision of the Governor General of India. This agent also provided overall direction and supervision to the nineteen princely states and the two zamindaris. Mewar was one of these princely states and Suwana, which fell in Bhilwara district, was governed by the princely state of Mewar, headed by the Maharana of Udaipur.

The British had maintained their monopoly over the opium trade in India. With the assistance of local intermediaries, who helped consolidate the supplies from cultivators, they acquired opium, purified and branded it, and exported it to China. It was under these conditions that Budhsingh, and later his son Kajorimal, had been able to create a flourishing opium business and a good life for themselves and their family. They would buy opium from small cultivators and sell it to the British.

Beginning in the last decade of the nineteenth century, the British had come under pressure at home as well as in India to discontinue the opium trade. But in the end, it was the Ten Years' Agreement between the British and China, concluded in 1907, which brought an end to the trade in 1917. Kajorimal and his family directly felt the repercussions of the phased end to British exports of opium from India.

As opium exports tapered off and anti-opium pressures continued to grow, the British began putting an end to their opium operations in India. In Mewar, the British agent advised the Maharana to ban the drug. That led the Maharana to send his representatives to seize opium wherever they could find it. This included the family storage of Kajorimal. The opium had been bought from cultivators on the promise of payment after it was sold to its final buyer, the British government. Preservation of the family reputation mandated that full payment be made to the cultivators. As the state of Mewar paid no compensation for the opium it had seized, Kajorimal was left with no choice but to sell all the family gold and silver jewellery to pay what he owed to the cultivators. That spelt the beginning of the end of the family.

Following Ugamchand's death in 1913, the family saw three more deaths: those of the wives of Kajorimal and Ugamchand, and of Kajorimal himself, who fell victim to the Spanish influenza in 1917. With all the senior members gone in four years' time, the responsibility of the family fell on the tender shoulders of seventeen-year-old Rajmal. His nephew Kanakmal was the same age as him, but being junior in status, he did not have the same level of responsibility. The only thing going for Rajmal at the time was that two years earlier he had been wedded to Dhapubai, a strong-willed woman who could stand by him like a rock.

Rajmal's first challenge was to host several community feasts to mark the deaths of the deceased on a scale commensurate with the 'status' of the family. With opium trade banned and the banking business having collapsed, the family had hardly any financial resources left to pay for these expensive events. They quickly went from being creditors to debtors.

Assisted by Kanakmal, Rajmal carried the family forward with the limited income he could generate from the agricultural land that the family still owned and small business activities on the side. As the years passed, Dhapubai gave birth to four children. The first two, both daughters, did not survive for very long. One died at the age of three and the other at one. It was under these circumstances that Rajmal and Dhapubai vowed that if their third child happened to be male, they would not cut his hair but keep it plaited for five years and offer it to Balaji of Sindri. Their wish came true.

On 30 June 1921, my father was born. Rajmal and Dhapubai named him Baloo Lal. Translated into English, the name meant 'son of Balaji'. In those days the birth of a male child, especially after two female children, would have been an occasion for a big celebration. But given the financial condition of the family, nothing of the sort happened. As per their vow, the parents kept my father's hair in a plait, offering it to Balaji five years later.

That tradition has been continued in our family. The first male child in the family is given his first haircut at the temple of Balaji of Sindri. When our eldest son, Hirsh, was born in October 1983, we lived in the United States. One of the earliest instructions I received from my mother after giving her the news of his birth was that we should not cut his hair till our next visit to India. We followed her wish. Hirsh's hair happened to grow unusually fast. Therefore, by the time we could finally visit India the following summer, his hair had to be tied up in a rubber band. I am sure he must have felt doubly relieved in the summer heat of Rajasthan once we took him to Sindri and had his head shaved!

In 1924, three years after the birth of my father, Dhapubai gave birth to a daughter who would be my bhua (father's sister). She was named Sajjan Kumari. Unlike their older sisters, my father and this younger sister would prove remarkably resilient and enjoy rich and long lives. My father would live to be almost eighty-five, breathing his last on 1 January 2006. Sajjan Kumari would live longer still, passing away in October 2019 at ninety-five years of age.

As Rajmal began getting a grip over the financial condition of the family, his big worry was to get a bride for his nephew Kanakmal. By 1926, the latter was twenty-six years old, a rather advanced age for someone to be still a bachelor in those days. Indeed, by the standards of the time, even his younger brothers, who were twenty-two and fifteen years old, were considered to be of marriageable age. However, given Rajmal's weak financial condition, no family was willing to offer their daughter in marriage to Kanakmal. The only option Rajmal had was to either pay a hefty amount in 'reet' to the family of the prospective bride, or let Kanakmal remain a bachelor. Reet was the reverse of the more familiar custom of dowry. It entailed the family of the groom 'gifting' a handsome sum of money to the family of the bride.

As a good Samaritan, Rajmal chose the first of these options, paying a large sum of money to a prominent family that agreed to marry one of its daughters to Kanakmal. The marriage took place in 1926. Rajmal spent well beyond his means on the wedding ceremony in the hope that this would entice other families into giving their daughters in marriage to the two younger brothers of Kanakmal. Sadly, no family took the bait, and the two brothers remained bachelors for life. On top of that, Rajmal had to sell or mortgage a significant proportion of the family's agricultural land and a part of the house to repay the loans he had taken to finance Kanakmal's lavish wedding. His gamble thus failed.

For Dhapubai, a bigger tragedy awaited. Within forty-five days of Kanakmal's wedding, Rajmal fell seriously ill and died. It was as if he had been living just long enough to get his nephew married. It seemed like the end of the world for Dhapubai. The first thing she had to do was to give away whatever jewellery she had to Kanakmal for hosting the community feast to commemorate the death of her husband. Even though the feast was held on a modest scale, it ended up depriving her of what every woman in India considers to be the last source of her personal financial security.

By convention, the oldest son becomes the 'heir' upon the death of his father. In those days, this succession was done via a formal 'pagari' ceremony, in which the pagari or turban of the father was tied on the head of the son. Accordingly, my father, only five years old at the time, was formally recognized as the head of his family. It is an event he distinctly remembered all his life, despite being so very young at the time. Writing in 1999, he recalled, 'The pagari of my father was tied on my head, recognizing me formally as his heir. I still have vivid memories of the events which took place in our family during those unfortunate days.'[2]

Kanakmal was now responsible for providing for the joint family, but found the task daunting. The family could barely get two square meals a day. His two younger brothers proved not to be of much help either. Worst of all, his wife and Dhapubai found it difficult to get along with each other.

In 1928, within two years of her husband's death, proud and strong-willed Dhapubai decided to part ways with Kanakmal's wife, separating all her affairs from those of the latter's family. Kanakmal's youngest brother, now seventeen years old, decided to throw in his lot with my father's family. It is probable that he

---

2 B.L. Panagariya, *My Little World*, unpublished.

too did not find his sister-in-law congenial enough to remain with her family.

The bond between my father and this cousin, ten years his senior, would remain as strong as between any two brothers till the latter's death at fifty years of age in 1961. He would be 'Kaka Saheb' to my siblings and me, and the only family 'elder' we would get to know well. Our grandparents from both our parents' sides were all gone before we were born. During summers, when we would be dragged to Suwana with our mother, Kaka Saheb would get us copies of the Ramayana and the Mahabharata to read. We brothers would often quarrel over who would get to read the epics first at any given time. When the season was right, he would also take us to the family farm where he would treat us to freshly plucked roasted corn.

During the last three or four years of his life, Kaka Saheb fell periodically ill and came for treatment to Jaipur, where we all lived. Those visits by him provided us a true opportunity to bond with him. When he was out of hospital and recuperating at home, we would pester him to tell us stories. He was a great storyteller and we would listen to him spellbound. My older brother Ashok came to form a particularly strong bond with him. A lifelong bachelor, Kaka Saheb was also a great devotee of Hanuman. He had even established a Hanuman temple on the platform at the entrance of the tenth-century temple across from our family house in Suwana. The temple remains intact today.

Thinking back, given Kaka Saheb's illness, my father must have anticipated his death. That was perhaps the reason a photographer was called home to photograph the family with him. One of those photographs remained hung in the family room of our home till the passing away of my mother in 2015. Though my father never expressed it, I am sure he always had a special place for this cousin in his heart. His death was my first close encounter with death, even though I was kept out of his funeral procession and cremation. My parents considered my older brother Ashok and me still too young to be exposed to a funeral and sent us to the place of a family friend. We found out about his passing only when my oldest brother, Ravi, came to take us back home after the cremation.

Dhapubai, her two children and Kaka Saheb, who had now become a part of her family, had no means of support except a small piece of agricultural land, which could partially meet their requirements of food grain. To generate some income, she sent Kaka Saheb to her parents' village, where he opened a small grocery shop with financial help from her brother. She herself began spending some six hours each day on the spinning wheel, which generated an income of one-eighth of a rupee. The petty amount she and her nephew earned was insufficient for even their bare subsistence. According to my father, more often than not the family had their meals without lentils or other accompaniments. They saw ghee or sugar only during festivals.

There was no school in Suwana at the time. As luck would have it – and luck, both good and bad, would play hide and seek throughout my father's life – in 1928, a seventy-year-old teacher came to Suwana and started a makeshift school in a rent-free house. He set a fee of one rupee per child per month. Dhapubai could hardly afford this fee. Yet, she must have had some sense that education could be valuable for my father and that he had nobody at home from whom to learn even the basics of language and arithmetic. Whatever her reasoning, what is known is that she took the plunge and sent him to the school, which had a dozen other students. Remarkably, the children came from diverse communities, ranging from Brahmin to Rajput to Jat to Jain to Dalit.

But within a few months, Dhapubai found that with less than four rupees per month, which she earned toiling on the spinning wheel, she was unable to keep up with the payment of the school fee. She had no choice but to pull my father out of the school. A month later, the teacher reconsidered his fee and agreed to take my father back at a fee of half a rupee per month. My father rejoined, and within a year managed to learn to read and write and solve simple arithmetical problems. At this point, the parents of a few of the other students decided that their children had learned enough and pulled them out of the school. That made the venture unviable for the teacher, who closed the school and left the village.

A few months passed, and a new teacher with some knowledge of English arrived in the village. Once again, he successfully collected a dozen students to start a school. My father was able to join the school and got a chance to learn elementary English alongside some more Hindi and arithmetic. But this school too failed to last very long. The teacher's extra-curricular activities came under the scanner of the village elders, who asked him to quietly leave the village.

The year was now 1931 and my father was ten years old. Dhapubai could take pride in having educated him enough during the preceding three years to read and write letters in Hindi and read telegrams in English. It was more than what most villagers could do in those days. At this juncture, a cloth merchant in Bhilwara offered my father a job that would pay three rupees per month and free meals. For a family struggling to make ends meet, this was an attractive offer, and Dhapubai was agreeable to my father taking up the job.

But before Father could begin the job, a relative of Dhapubai, who was a teacher in a school in the town of Banera, came to Suwana. He recognized my father's capabilities and advised Dhapubai to send him to Banera for further studies. It so happened that only a few days earlier, Dhapubai had received a message from her sister in Banera urging her to send her young son to her to study further in the middle school in her town. Some years ago, the sister had been married into another Panagariya family, not directly related to ours, living in Banera. At the time, Dhapubai had not taken her sister's suggestion seriously. But the advice from a teacher from the very school in which her son would be studying had an altogether different effect on her.

The choice must have been a difficult one for Dhapubai. Bhilwara was only three miles away. Her son could continue to live in Suwana and commute to work. This way, he would be by her side and available to help her, especially in any emergency situation. Furthermore, the job there would bring an income almost equal to what she herself earned. Banera, on the other hand, was twelve miles away, and if my father went there, she would only be able to see him during the summer vacations. With her nephew Kaka Saheb already in her parents' village, she would be left alone at home with her daughter.

Yet, to her credit, Dhapubai opted for educating her son further. For a woman who in all likelihood had never gone to school, this must have been not just a difficult decision but a daring one, a gamble of sorts. Apart from the prospect of missing her son through most of the year except during the two summer months, the thought of his twelve-mile journey from Suwana to Banera on his own, with no means to find out for many days whether he had safely reached his destination, must have been terrifying. The strength to make that decision must have come principally from the conviction that education would secure the future of her only son, and from her faith in the values she had instilled in him. Whether or not she thought in these terms, this single decision of hers, in retrospect, turned out to be the most critical turning point in not just the life of my father but that of all subsequent generations of the family.

The school in Banera was to begin on 1 July 1931. To maximize his time with his mother and yet arrive in Banera on time to begin his studies, my father set out for the twelve-mile journey on foot at 5 a.m. on 30 June 1931. By coincidence, this was his birthday and he had turned ten that day. It took him ten hours to cover the distance. It must have been a huge relief when he finally arrived at the home of his mausi and mausa (aunt and uncle) at 3 p.m. The two received him warmly as if he was their own son.

The following day, my father was admitted to the fourth grade in Akshaya Memorial Hindi Middle School. Though he was of the right age for this grade, his readiness for it was questionable. He had never studied in a proper school and had had no exposure at all to the subjects of history and geography, which were an integral part of the fourth-grade curriculum. When it came to mathematics, while he had been good at arithmetics, he had no knowledge of geometry. His class teacher advised him to move to a lower grade. But the teacher on whose advice Dhapubai had sent him to Banera intervened to ensure that he was retained in the fourth grade. Father soon proved that he was up to the challenge. He ranked second in his class in the half-yearly examinations, and then got the top rank in the annual examinations.

The move to Banera was to be transformational for my father. This was in no small measure due to the fact that the town offered him an environment and opportunity to grow that Suwana, perhaps even Bhilwara, could not have. Situated in the midst of the Aravalli mountain ranges, Banera was a picturesque town. Though it declined over time and came to be formally designated a village, with a population of 11,400 in 2011, it was a hub of activity during the years my father studied there. The town came into prominence in 1681 when Mughal Emperor Aurangzeb conferred the rights to seventy-five surrounding villages, inclusive of Banera, on Raja Bhim Singh, the fourth son of Maharana Raj Singh I of Mewar. Because of this conferment, Bhim Singh is also often referred to as the founder of Banera. By the time the great-grandson of Bhim Singh came to the helm in Banera, the Mughal empire had disintegrated. At that point, suzerainty of Banera passed on to Mewar state.

During the years my father studied in Banera, it had a population of approximately 7,000. Unlike most jagirdars of Mewar, the rulers of Banera were progressive and enlightened. They built numerous irrigation tanks in their jagir, among other things, which added to the prosperity of farmers while also bringing extra revenue to them. Because of the enlightened policies of its rulers, Banera remained free of any agrarian unrest through its entire existence of almost three centuries.

The rulers made good use of the revenues they received. They added beautiful palaces to the old Banera Fort on the hill, for which the town is known even today. They constructed a large tank and a massive swimming pool on the outskirts of the town while building a beautiful park adjacent to it. The Akshaya Memorial School was built in 1903, and an allopathic dispensary in 1925. Even the major towns of Mewar, such as Bhilwara and Chittor, did not have allopathic dispensaries in those days.

The ruling family encouraged sports. The town had an impressive playground in a beautiful, natural setting outside the walled town. Students, teachers and others regularly played football and hockey there. There were two volleyball playgrounds adjacent to the school. The games were mandatory for students, with punishment being meted out to those found absent from them. The town hosted inter-school and inter-town tournaments, which attracted large crowds and created much excitement all around. The traditional rivalry between Banera and the nearby town of Shahpura found expression on the playground as well.

The annual school day was celebrated with great fanfare. On that day, there were inter-class tournaments in traditional games such as kabaddi and kho-kho by day, while the main function took place in the evening, with the rajadhiraj presiding. The function included one-act plays, dances and music by students. The programme concluded with prizes distributed to winners in the sports events and the year's examination toppers. My father never won a prize in sports, but he never missed one in studies. The tradition set by him has been upheld at least in part by those of us who have followed him: not a single member of the Panagariya family has distinguished himself or herself in any sport to date!

Returning to the main story, my father had successfully overcome the initial handicaps of insufficient preparation for the fourth grade and topped his class in the final examinations. The academic year over, summer vacations began, and Father got the opportunity to return home. Dhapubai had been looking forward to this day since he had left Suwana almost ten months earlier. Over his protests, she saw to it that she supplemented his diet with ghee and milk during the months he was with her. He got to enjoy his summer break with his former classmates and friends. During the year in Banera, he had gained exposure to stories of the Mahatma Gandhi-led freedom movement against the British. Inspired by those stories, he would often go around the village with his friends shouting the slogan *'Mahatma Gandhi ki jai!'*, an act forbidden by the Mewar state government under direction from its British agent. The presence of a government official within hearing distance would be a special reason for Father and his friends to raise the slogan. Luckily, no official took any action against the children.

Before my father and his mother knew it, the summer vacation months flew and it was time for him to return to school for another year of study. Dhapubai bid her son goodbye with tears in her eyes. Once in Banera, he resumed his studies. His first rank in the fourth grade earned him free books for the fifth grade from Rajadhiraj Amar Singh. The school had a public-spirited scoutmaster, and at his encouragement Father joined scouting. The town also had a good library, which Father began visiting on a daily basis. He would regularly read the Hindi newspaper *Veer Arjun,* which the library subscribed to. It was edited by lndra Vidyavachaspati, a leading journalist known for his nationalist writings. The paper inculcated the spirit of nationalism in my father from an early age.

Given that Banera had two small water tanks and one big tank, even the small children in the town knew how to swim. In his twelfth year now, my father still lacked the skill. He decided to teach himself to swim. He borrowed a couple of inflated tubes from a friend, went to one of the tanks situated in the middle of the town, and jumped into it with the tubes. It so happened that the tubes floated away and he began to drown. By the grace of God, an expert swimmer happened to be watching him. He immediately jumped into the tank and saved him. Though my father eventually did learn to swim, it was an escape he never forgot the rest of his life and he would always describe it as a miracle.

Father managed to stay at the top of his class in the fifth-grade examinations too. The school was once again closed for the summer vacation and he returned to Suwana to be with his mother and friends. During this visit, he got to learn astrology from a former classmate's father, who had several books on the subject, including the *Bhrigusamhita*. In retrospect, judging by how well Father assessed the personalities of my children, Hirsh and Ajay, from their horoscopes, and predicted the broad contours of their future, he had mastered the subject well. Amita, my wife, still marvels at the accuracy of his assessments and predictions. He also read the Ramayana and the Mahabharata during the summer, finding the latter particularly fascinating.

The year was now 1933 and my father and his sister were twelve and nine years old, respectively. Kanakmal's younger brother was twenty-nine and still a bachelor. Kanakmal's wife and some of the local Oswal families began pressing Dhapubai to offer her daughter in exchange for a bride for him. However, Dhapubai was a shrewd and tough woman who knew how to guard her own interests. She understood perfectly well that her pretty daughter was her only chance to get a bride for her own son. She firmly ignored the entreaties of her sister-in-law (Kanakmal's wife) and the Oswal families. Nevertheless, in order not to leave matters to chance, she decided to move fast to arrange matches for her son and daughter.

I do not know how she went about connecting with families of potential matches. It is probable that her brother's family helped her. What I do know from conversations with my bhua is that she worked out a triangular arrangement with two other families that had a brother-sister pair each. As per the deal, the three brother-sister pairs would be simultaneously matched into three husband-wife pairs and be married in quick succession.

My father and bhua made the first brother-sister pair. My mother and her older brother made the second pair. And Bhuralal Khatod, who would marry my bhua, and his sister made the third pair. The families of the three pairs agreed that my bhua would be married to Bhuralal Khatod first; his sister would then be married to my mother's brother; and the last would be my mother to marry my father. The sequence was on the insistence of Bhuralal's family; they feared that if my father got married before my bhua was given to their son, Dhapubai might go back on her word. The agreed sequence naturally placed all the risk on my grandmother's shoulders, but given the circumstances, she took the chance.

Formal engagement ceremonies for the three couples were performed during the summer of 1933. The first two marriages took place within the year. The marriage of my father and mother was fixed for the summer of 1934. My mother, Mohan Kumari, and her family lived in Bhilwara, as did Bhuralal and his family. Therefore, while my bhua went from a village to a town, my mother migrated in the reverse direction. The latter was only two or three months younger than my father. At the time of marriage, they were both thirteen years old.

On 1 July 1933, my father was back in his school in Banera. He continued to do well at studies and retained the top rank in the sixth grade as well. When the school closed for the summer, he was back in Suwana in the third week of May 1934. Ceremonies for his marriage, which lasted nearly a month, began almost immediately. Every single day, relatives, family friends and neighbours in the village would invite him for meals. 'Sometimes I had to eat at about a dozen places in a single day,' he recalled in his autobiography. Every evening, there would be singing and dancing at home, and every third or fourth day he would be taken on horseback in a procession around the village. For Dhapubai, this must have been one of the happiest months of her life.

This happiness was punctured, however, the day before the marriage party was to leave for Bhilwara, where the wedding was to take place. Some time back, the Oswal community of Bhilwara had got divided into two camps, with one camp supporting community feasts to commemorate deaths and the other opposing it. The Oswal community of Suwana had joined the former camp while my mother's family was in the latter camp.

The night before the wedding party was to leave, the panchas (leaders) of the Oswal community in Suwana informed Dhapubai and her family that they would join the party only on condition that their meals in Bhilwara were arranged at a place other than the bride's home. This being entirely contrary to the longstanding tradition, an effort was made to get the panchas to change their mind. Discussions continued for several hours during the night. In the end, at 4 a.m., Dhapubai relented and the wedding party left for Bhilwara at 6 a.m. But once in Bhilwara, the panchas upped the ante, demanding that the procession of the groom's wedding party not pass by the bride's house. Given the prevailing custom, that would have been insulting to my mother's family. Rather than accept such humiliation, my father and other members of his extended family refused to bow to the demand. The panchas and the other Oswal families returned to Suwana without participating in the wedding.

Luckily, an Oswal wedding party from Sanganer, where another branch of our family still lived, happened to be around for another marriage ceremony. They offered to merge their party with whatever remained of my father's wedding party. The combined party then went past the houses of both brides, thereby saving my father's family from embarrassment.

The wedding ceremonies lasted for three days, after which my father returned to Suwana. Given that marriages in those days took place when the bride and groom were still young, the bride would not move to her husband's family immediately after the wedding. Accordingly, my mother stayed in Bhilwara with her parents.

In Mewar, in those days, only men used to form the wedding party of the groom. Therefore, Dhapubai had stayed back while the wedding party went to Bhilwara for the ceremony. Upon his return, Father discovered that his mother was furious at the humiliation that the panchas of the Oswal community of Suwana had inflicted on her family. She vowed that she would not accept even water offered by any of them for the rest of her life. A proud woman, she remained firm in her resolve for the remainder of the one and a half years of her life. The terminal illness that was to strike her soon did not break her will. Elderly women from the Oswal families would bring her buttermilk during her illness but she would steadfastly refuse it. She would swallow roti with water, if that was the alternative, rather than accept offerings from those families.

Soon after his marriage, my father's summer vacation ended and he returned to Banera to resume his studies for another year. He was to now appear for the Hindi Middle Examination conducted by the Allahabad Board of Vernacular Final Departmental Examinations. Because all the students from his school had failed in the examination the previous year, the teachers as well as the students were under great pressure to do better this time around. The rajadhiraj of Banera had threatened that he would sack all the teachers of the school if the story of the previous year repeated itself.

The examination was held in March 1935 in Ajmer and the class did well, with everyone passing it. My father proved himself to be the best student in the class once again. He was the only one to pass in the second division with distinction (high honours) in mathematics. He was the first student to get a distinction in any subject since the Middle School had been established in 1903. The rajadhiraj of Banera and his prime minister awarded him a gold medal each for the accomplishment. My brother Ravi still has one of these gold medals in his possession. According to him, my father had exchanged the other gold medal for books.

The visit Father got to make to Ajmer to take the board examination was the most fascinating trip of his life until then. That was the first time he got to travel on a train. There were other students and a teacher who accompanied them. The train arrived at Ajmer railway station in the evening, and Father saw electric lights for the first time. From the railway station, they went to Soniji ki Dharmshala (a charitable inn where travellers can stay temporarily at nominal or no charge), where he encountered water coming out of a tap, again for the first time. After settling down in the place, the students devoted the following two days to preparation for the examination, which was scheduled for the third day. Once the examination was over, they visited some prominent spots in Ajmer, such as Soniji Ki Nasiyan (a Hindu temple), Dhai

Din ka Jhopra (a twelfth-century mosque) and Khwaja Saheb ki Dargah (a Sufi shrine). My father later recalled that throughout that trip he thought Ajmer was nothing short of a fairyland.

After returning from Ajmer, Father came straight to Suwana. It had been a year since his marriage and it was time for my mother to join his family. Accordingly, Dhapubai sent him to Bhilwara, where he spent a fortnight before returning home with my mother. Much to his horror, upon his return he discovered that his mother had fallen ill during his absence. At the time, he thought it was some ordinary fever from which she would recover soon. But with the passage of time, bit by bit, his hopes began to fade away.

Summer over, Father returned to Banera to figure out his Future. Three of his classmates and he decided that they should take the Mewar Middle Examination in English, which would make them eligible for admission to the ninth grade, as per the rules of the Mewar Board of High School. The headmaster of their Middle School in Banera encouraged them and even agreed to give them free lessons.

Though he began preparing for the examination in earnest, Father remained distracted on account of his mother's illness. Restless, he returned to Suwana a month later, only to find her entirely bedridden. There had been no improvement whatsoever in her condition. Nevertheless, Dhapubai insisted that she would be fine and sent him back to Banera to resume his studies.

A few months later, Dhapubai's brother came to Suwana and took her to his hometown Balesaria, hoping that the blessings of the local deity would cure her. My father also went from Banera to Balesaria to join her. He was shattered to see the deterioration in her health. She was, in fact, suffering from tuberculosis. Years of hard work, malnutrition and unending family worries had left her too weak to fight this dreaded disease. As my father would recall later, 'At the time, there was no cure for this nasty disease. And even if there had been one, we could hardly afford it.'

Dhapubai stayed in Balesaria for a month, visiting the local deity twice a week. But her health continued to deteriorate. My father brought her back to Suwana. Gradually, she was reduced to a skeleton. As death approached, she told my father that after she was gone, he should invite the local Oswal families to the community feast to commemorate her death and break the impasse between them and our family. Perhaps she felt that after her death, my father would need the support of the community. At 4 p.m. on 26 January 1936, this grand grandmother of mine breathed her last.

This must have been the most devastating event of my father's life. When his father died, he was only five years old and may not have realized the gravity of the event. Besides, his mother, the ultimate source of security for a child, was still there for him. But at fourteen, he must have had an appreciation of what it would mean to be entirely on his own. To her credit, Dhapubai had seen to it that he had acquired enough education to stand on his feet and that he had his life companion, my mother, with him before she departed. But at least at that time, none of this could have been much consolation to my father. Indeed, judging by what he wrote more than sixty years later in his autobiography, it was not. To quote him,

> I was made to light the pyre at the cremation place on the banks of the village tank. I was shaken. Within hours mother was reduced to ashes. Having lost my father at the age of five, she was not only a mother to me but a father as well. She was a strict disciplinarian and never bent before anybody in the worst

> of circumstances. She gave me only one advice during her long illness, that I should remain honest and truthful. Her memory always inspired me to remain so.[3]

The advice his mother gave from her deathbed would become the guiding principle of my father's life. He would remain truthful and honest throughout his life and eventually hardwire all his children to remain so too. Only once in his life would he resort to a harmless lie so that he could continue his studies. Though his mother would have likely approved of the lie, given the circumstances that led to it, the fact of having deviated from the promise made to her would bother my father every once in a while in his later life.

---

3 B.L. Panagariya, *My Little World*, unpublished.

2

My Father – On His Own at Fourteen

I WAS BORN IN 1952. After completing a master's degree in Jaipur, I left for the United States to do a PhD in economics at Princeton University. The plan was to return to India after completing the degree, but that did not happen. Instead, upon completion of the degree in 1978, I joined the faculty of the department of economics of the University of Maryland at College Park, located on the outskirts of Washington, DC. I married Amita in India in 1981, and became an associate professor with tenure at Maryland in 1983.

In 1985, my father and mother visited us. This was their only visit to the country. By this time, both our children, Hirsh and Ajay, had been born. During the six weeks that Father and Mother spent with us, we travelled extensively on the East Coast of the United States. During one of these outings to Washington, DC, as we were passing by the White House, Father remarked with a touch of pride how I, at such a young age, had successfully made it from the capital of the state of Rajasthan in India to the capital of the world. I replied that it was his journey from Suwana to Jaipur that represented a far bigger leap than my migration from Jaipur to the United States. For, once he had arrived in Jaipur, the road to the United States for me was an easy one. Thinking back, my response had greatly understated the contrast between our two journeys. Compared with the hazardous course he had had to cover between his mother's funeral pyre and eventual arrival in Jaipur, where I was born, my journey from Jaipur to the United States was more like a joyride.

Returning to Father's journey to Jaipur then, it may be recalled that my grandmother's last wish was that he should commemorate her death with a community feast at which the Oswal families of Suwana would be invited. Accordingly, my father hosted the feast on the appointed day and invited the families. But even on this delicate occasion, the panchas representing the community did not miss the opportunity to extract a price. Many years earlier, a silver crown of a statue of Parshvanath, one of the twenty-four founders of the Jain religion, had been stolen, among other valuables from my father's family, in a burglary that took place at the family house in Suwana. As a condition for joining the feast, the panchas demanded that the family pay for the restoration of the crown. Eager to fulfil the last wish of his mother, my father and others in the extended family agreed to put up with yet another insult in a series of insults that the panchas had inflicted on the family, especially on my grandmother, during the preceding two years.

But the humiliations had reached a breaking point. Even at the young age of fourteen, my father concluded that the system of community panchayats had not just hurt many families irreparably but had also damaged the community as a whole. He resolved that when he came of age he would do everything in his power to put an end to it. Later, after acquiring an official position in the newly formed state of Rajasthan, when he became the de facto head of the family, he saw to it that all ceremonies at the wedding of his nephew, Kanakmal's son, were conducted without any consultation with the community panchayat. That act of his heralded the beginning of the end of the power that the community panchayat had exercised for decades. Within a matter of years, the system withered away.

The period of bereavement over, my father returned to Banera to begin preparing for the English language examination that was to take place in Udaipur in March 1936. Preparations done, he along with other students went to Udaipur two days prior to the examination. Since this was their first visit to Udaipur, they stayed three extra days after the examination and went sightseeing.

Known as the City of Lakes, Udaipur is a beautiful place. Father and others in the party visited tourist spots such as the City Palace, the Sajjan Niwas garden and the many lakes around the city. The festival of Gangaur happened to coincide with their visit. In those days, Udaipur celebrated it with a procession that was led by Maharana Bhupal Singh, his ministers and senior officials. That formed a special attraction for my father and his classmates. Later that evening, they also got to see the spectacular boat procession in the famous Lake Pichola and beautiful fireworks. After an exciting visit, they returned to Banera. From Banera, my father came straight to Suwana, where he got to tell the stories of his Udaipur visit for several days to spellbound audiences.

The examination results came in June, and my father turned out to be the only student from Banera to pass it. He was now eligible to join the ninth grade in school, but had no means to finance his further studies. Therefore, he returned to Banera to seek the advice of his teachers and elders.

One of his teachers and the headmaster of the school advised my father to continue his studies. The former went out of his way and travelled with him to Udaipur to get him admitted to Maharana College in the ninth grade. He also got him a room and boarding in the Jain hostel there, where other out-of-town students of the college stayed. As if that was not enough, he then took him to a businessman belonging to the Oswal community to secure some financial assistance for him. The businessman generously agreed to cover half of the fee charged by the Jain hostel.

Unfortunately, the teacher did not live long after that. He died in an accident a few years later. My father felt deeply saddened by his sudden passing away. He remained grateful to this teacher all his life. Describing him as 'a jewel among men', he later recalled, 'But for him, I would have rusted in some dark corner as a teacher at a school or as a munim (accountant) in a grocery shop.'

While half of my father's hostel fee was now covered, there still remained the other half. In addition, he needed to finance the cost of books, tuition and other college fees and living expenses. The prince of Banera, who lived in Udaipur at the time, paid for his books. The principal of the college generously exempted him from tuition and other fees. For the remaining expenses, he found a part-time job as a tutor to a young lady from a well-to-do family. It was as if all the forces of nature had come together to see him study further.

In the hostel, my father was placed in a double room, paired with a tenth-grade student named Satya Deo Sharma. Sharma came from a well-to-do family in Bhilwara and was studying science. The two formed a lasting friendship that eventually extended to the next generation. Sharma went on to become an eye surgeon, and we came to address him as 'Dr Saheb'. It was to his home that my brother Ashok and I were sent the day Kaka Saheb died. At the time, he was working at the SMS Hospital in Jaipur as a doctor while also teaching at the attached SMS Medical College. He lived to be ninety-nine and passed away only in January 2019.

Lacking any guidance, my father had chosen history and geography for his electives. Hindi, English and mathematics were required courses. Later, he would acquire a background in law and, in the early 1950s, go on to do an LLB degree. He went on to top the entire university in his LLB examinations, winning the gold medal for it.

Most students covered the two-kilometre distance between the hostel and college on their bicycles. My father could not afford such a luxury. So he did what he had always done: walk. He calibrated his departure from the hostel and his walking speed carefully to be sure that he never arrived late for his first class. Each evening, after returning from college, he would visit the nearby Theosophical Society Lodge and read the *Hindustan Times* available there. That helped him gain fluency in English, a skill that was scarce in those days and came in handy later. Reading the newspaper on a daily basis also made him the best-informed student in the class. Because of this, the other students in his class would often call him 'Radio'.

The final examinations for the ninth grade took place in April 1937. My father managed to top his class of forty. He was off to a good start in college, where he would compete with more select students than in Banera. With the onset of the summer vacations, he got a chance to return to Suwana. As the first person from the village to go to a big city to study, he now got to hold court on the grand platform outside the family house where his great-grandfather Budhsingh had once settled disputes among the villagers. Fellow villagers, young and old, gathered around this sixteen-year-old to hear him talk about life in the city of Udaipur, its Maharana, and the events taking place in India and the world. They would be in awe of him and ask whether he was studying so much to become the 'thaar babu' (telegraph clerk) or patwari (a village official who maintains land records). The simple village folk could not imagine that a fellow villager of theirs could go any further than these mighty ranks.

Among other things, my father told his audience stories of the freedom movement that Mahatma Gandhi was leading against the British. He also told them about other leading figures in the freedom movement, such as Jawaharlal Nehru and Sardar Vallabhbhai Patel. The village folk would listen to him with rapt attention, though they would occasionally express doubt as to whether Mahatma Gandhi would ever be able to throw the mighty British out of the country. Nevertheless, the stories he told created a great deal of goodwill for the Congress in the hearts of the village people. A good number, especially among the young, began to develop feelings of nationalism. 'They were ready to do anything that I wanted them to do, though at this stage I myself did not know what to do,' my father recalled later. Some, including a sixty-five-year-old man, began wearing clothes made of khadi (home-spun coarse cloth).

A year earlier, during the summer of 1936, my father and his friends had successfully persuaded their fellow villagers to end the age-old practice of offering male goats and male buffaloes in sacrifice to the community gods. Emboldened by that experience, the following summer they pushed for an end to the practices of child marriage and community feasts to commemorate deaths. But this time around they failed miserably on both counts. On child marriage, the villagers argued that they were able to economize on expenses by conducting the marriage of several children simultaneously. Moreover, married girls joined their husbands only after they had attained puberty. On community feasts commemorating deaths, they agreed that the practice had ruined many families, but were not willing to come forward to end it.

After the summer vacation my father returned to Udaipur. He was now in the tenth grade. He and Dr Saheb (Satya Deo Sharma) once again became roommates in the hostel. Classes began, and he was back to the familiar routine. Soon came the month of September, when it was time for the tenth-grade students to fill in their application forms for the board examinations to be conducted by the Board of High School and Intermediate Examinations, Ajmer, in March 1938.

The application form had to be accompanied by a fee of Rs 25. My father did not have such a large sum of money and did not know whom he could get it from. Therefore, though he completed the form, he could not submit it. Two days remained till the deadline and he still did not know what to do about the fee. It looked as if the efforts of his teacher from Banera and his own hard work during the preceding one and a half years would all be in vain. The prospect of ending up without a high school diploma loomed large.

That night, my father went to bed deeply depressed and worried. But he suddenly woke up at 3 a.m. with the thought that he should try his luck with Tej Singh Mehta, a minister in the princely state of Mewar. The minister lived in a bungalow not far from his hostel. He had nothing to lose: the worst-case scenario was that the minister would send him back empty-handed. Though my father had neither seen the minister nor knew anyone who could provide an introduction to him, he took courage and arrived at the bungalow at 7 a.m. the next day. A big crowd had already gathered there to seek favours from the minister.

At about 8 a.m., a tall man emerged from the house. The entire crowd stood up and saluted the gentleman. My father did the same. Assuming that he was the minister, my father sought his attention as he walked past and pleaded with him to sanction him Rs 25 to cover his examination fee. The man pulled out a one-rupee coin from his pocket and placed it in my father's palm. That was of no use to Father, and so he returned it to the man with thanks. It looked like the game was over. Dejected, he was about to begin walking back to his hostel when he heard someone say that the man whom they had just seen was Mohan Singh Mehta, the younger brother of Tej Singh Mehta. Father immediately stopped in his tracks and heaved a sigh of relief; he still had a fighting chance.

Minister Tej Singh Mehta came out at about 9 a.m. Everyone saluted him, and he began listening to the plight of his audience, one by one. When my father's turn came, he explained to him how his future depended on being able to pay the twenty-five-rupee fee. The minister told him to submit an application to him, which Father promptly did. The minister neither gave him an assurance of assistance nor ruled it out. Father returned to the hostel and immediately left for college to arrive in time for his first class.

Because my father was a good student, the principal of the school called him into his office and asked him why he had not submitted his examination form yet. Father told him that he planned to do it the next day, which was the last date for submission of the form. He remained worried throughout the day. His friends only added to his anxiety, telling him not to expect much from the minister. The likes of them, they reasoned, helped only their own kith and kin, not ordinary citizens. This was not without basis: as we will see later, the entire system of the Mewar government was based on patronage and nepotism rather than merit.

The long day passed and the next one came. My father went to college with disappointment written all over his face. As usual, he arrived on time and began his classes. At 11 a.m., the school principal came to the class and asked him to accompany him to his office. Father did, and in what would remain one of the most pleasant surprises of all his life, he found a messenger of the Mewar government waiting for him, with not just Rs 25 but Rs 40, under orders from Minister Tej Singh Mehta.

With a big sigh of relief, my father received the money, gave a receipt to the messenger and submitted the examination form with the requisite fee. With the fifteen rupees that remained, he later bought clothes and shoes, which he had badly needed for some time. He felt eternally grateful to the minister. Sixty years later, he would reminisce in his autobiography, 'So there were great men like Shri (Mr) Tej Singh Mehta even in those times, who were prepared to help a needy student. Next morning, I went to Shri Mehta and thanked him profusely. He was pleased.'[4]

One would think that after this difficult trial, the path to taking the high school examination would be clear for my father. But the story did not end there. There was a rule at the time that anyone who had been married before eighteen years of age would not be permitted to appear for the high school examination. There was a question in the examination form asking the applicant whether he or she was married. Recognizing that the only way he would be allowed to take the examination was by answering the question in the negative, Father had checked the box that said no.

Unfortunately for him, before long the principal called him to his office and informed him that a student had filed a complaint saying that, contrary to my father's entry in the examination form, he was married. Confronted by the principal, Father immediately confessed that he had had no option but to take recourse to a lie to be able to take the examination. Aware that Father was one of the best students in his class and a most sincere one at that, the principal was taken aback. He immediately called the student who had lodged the complaint and asked him to withdraw it. The complainant complied, tearing his submission into several pieces on the spot.

Overcome with intense gratitude towards the principal, my father instantly fell at his feet. He was out of words to thank him. Recalling the incident in his autobiography, he later wrote, 'Perhaps Providence wanted that I should do my high school. No body except we three knew about the episode. I still regret I had to take resort to tell a lie, contrary to the advice given to me by my

---

4 Panagariya, *My Little World.*

mother from her deathbed.'[5] Evidently, the pain of having broken the promise to his mother even under perfectly understandable circumstances had remained with him all his life.

The high school examinations took place in March 1938 in Ajmer and lasted three weeks. The results came in June. My father passed in the second division. Out of a total of 125 students who had taken the examination from the college, only one passed in the first division. Father had been ahead of him in the final examination in the ninth grade, but their fortunes had reversed in the board examinations. But that is life!

For now, this was the end of my father's studies. He lacked the financial resources to study further. Moreover, it was high time that he shouldered the burden of providing for the family, especially for my mother, who had been living in the family house in Suwana with Kanakmal and his family all this while.

Soon after the examinations in Ajmer, my father returned to Suwana. Once the results came out, it was time for him to look for a job. Though he would face some difficulty finding a suitable position, it is fair to say that the toughest phase of his life was now over. He would experience the usual ups and downs of life but not the kind of trials he had gone through during the first seventeen years of his life.

5 Ibid.

3

Yearning to be Part of the Freedom Movement

BEFORE I NARRATE THE more pleasant part of my father's journey, it is necessary to digress briefly to describe the prevailing administrative system and political atmosphere in contemporary Mewar, of which Bhilwara and Suwana were constituents. As I briefly mentioned earlier, in the context of the family's opium business, broadly speaking, the British had divided India into two parts from an administrative viewpoint: a set of provinces that they administered directly; and numerous princely states, zamindaris and jagirdaris, which they let local hereditary rulers govern under the direction and supervision of a British agent.

A governor, lieutenant governor or chief commissioner administered the provinces, depending on their size. The system was strictly hierarchical, with the authority at each level being subordinate to the one directly above. Governors, lieutenant governors and chief commissioners were answerable to the governor general, who was in turn answerable to the British government in London. The British Parliament enacted the laws governing the provinces.

Princely states, frequently referred to as just 'states', were in a subsidiary relationship with the British Crown, whereby they were effectively vassals of the latter. They were not to make war or engage in negotiations with other states. Larger states had their own British resident, while the smaller ones were grouped into a number of agencies, with each having a British agent as the representative of the British government.

So long as the British resident or agent approved, local hereditary rulers of the states could maintain their own laws and governance systems internally. But the residents and agents became increasingly intrusive over time. They would often decide who the prime minister of the state would be and exercise control over the administrative system through the latter. At the time the British left, there were more than 560 princely states, as well as thousands of zamindaris and jagirdaris that were in relationships similar to those of the princely states with the Crown. Altogether, the states, zamindaris and jagirdaris accounted for approximately 40 per cent of India's land area and 23 per cent of its population.

After Independence, the Indian government created the current state of Rajasthan by amalgamating nineteen independent princely states, two chiefships and one centrally administered territory known as Ajmer-Merwara. The British government had exercised its control over these states and chiefships through its agent to the governor general, with his headquarters in Ajmer. Mewar state, also known as Udaipur state, was one of these princely states. Its ruler, known as the Maharana, and the secretariat, called the Mahakma Khas, were located in Udaipur.

Founded in the sixth century CE, Mewar was the oldest among all the princely states in India. According to the 1941 Census, it had a population of 2 million. For administrative purposes, the state was divided into sixteen districts. Each district was headed by a hakim, who was collector, superintendent of police and magistrate all rolled into one. In these capacities, he had the charge of land revenue collection, maintenance of law and order and administration of justice. Districts were sub-divided into several tehsils, each administered by a naib [assistant or deputy] hakim.

Till as late as the end of the 1930s, Mewar state had no civil or criminal procedure code. It even lacked the law of evidence. In administering justice, the hakims and naib hakims followed procedures established by practice or by what seemed convenient. Many gave judgements based on the bribes they could extract. In principle, the highest court of appeal was the mahendraj sabha (chief court), but in practice the Maharana could revise its judgment.

A handful of ministers ran the Mahakma Khas. A few clerks and orderlies assisted them. Official documents were written in the Mewari language using the Devanagari script. The ruler appointed the ministers, heads of departments and hakims from amongst the few 'mutsaddi' (noble) families, irrespective of their educational or other qualifications. As a result, many senior officers, including hakims, lacked the qualifications for the jobs they held.

In 1939, the British government appointed T. Vijayaraghavacharya, a former prime minister of Cochin state, as the prime minister of

Mewar. He reorganized the state secretariat along modern lines. He separated the executive and judiciary. He constituted a State Civil Service and a Subordinate Civil Service. He also codified civil and criminal law and established a High Court of Judicature, which replaced the old Mahendraj Sabha. Finally, he dismissed a number of corrupt, inefficient and uneducated officers from service.

It may seem curious that despite the feelings of nationalism that I mentioned my father inculcating within himself and his friends in Suwana, I have made no reference to any organized action by the Congress to draw these young men into the freedom movement. The answer to this puzzle is that until 1938, the Congress had explicitly limited its freedom movement to the eleven provinces directly ruled by the British. Under the Government of India Act of 1935, the British had decided to give autonomy to these provinces and held elections in them in 1936. The Congress had fought elections in all eleven provinces and successfully formed the government in eight. Similar elections did not take place in the princely states because local rulers ruled them. The Congress had made a conscious decision not to extend the freedom movement to the princely states, since seeking popularly elected governments there would bring it into direct conflict with the rulers, who were not foreign. Mahatma Gandhi was particularly reluctant to bring the Congress into conflict with the princes, whom he saw as friends rather than enemies.

As far as the people of the princely states were concerned, the direct cause of their misery originated in the exploitative policies of their immediate rulers rather than the British government, even though the local royalty ruled under the overall supervision of the latter. In the provinces and territories that the British directly ruled, the British Parliament enacted all the laws. But in the princely states, local kings and maharajas exercised that power. As such, popular movements in the princely states had been directed against the local rulers – focusing on issues such as land taxes, forced labour and misgovernment – rather than against the British. The role of the national freedom movement in the princely states was indirect, limited to imparting greater legitimacy to the local movements. These movements sought redress of the same grievances from local rulers in the princely states that the Congress did from the British government in the provinces and territories directly under it. A good example of local movements against rulers in Mewar was the Bijolia Kisan Movement from 1897 to 1941. Waged against excessive land taxes, forced labour and other excesses of the local rulers, this movement gave rise to leaders who later founded Mewar Praja Mandal, the organization that brought the region directly into the national freedom movement during its last phase. As I noted earlier, where rulers were just and good to the people, as in the case of Banera, no such local movement existed.

A turning point in the history of participation in the national movement by people from the princely states came in 1938. At its convention at Haripur in Orissa that year, the Congress modified its stance with respect to local movements in princely states. It adopted a resolution calling upon the subjects to launch their movements for responsible governments in their respective states. The resolution explicitly forbade the subjects from launching these movements under the name of the Congress, however. Therefore, the freedom movements in the princely states, which began in 1938, were launched under the auspices of Praja Mandals or Praja Parishads (people's associations).

No sooner had the Congress opened the door than the people in Mewar formed the Mewar Praja Mandal, with the objective of establishing a responsible government in the state. The founder of the organization was Manikya Lal Verma, a charismatic leader who had played a pivotal role in the famous Bijolia Kisan Movement. Later, after Independence, he went on to serve as a member of the Constituent Assembly of India and as prime minister of the United State of Rajasthan (USR), which was formed by merging Mewar with the other southern and southeastern princely states of Rajputana in April 1948. My father would later directly connect with Verma and edit the official weekly newspaper of the Mewar Praja Mandal just prior to the formation of the USR. But that episode is still a few years away from where I must now resume his story.

With a high school diploma in hand, my father thought that his life would be smooth henceforth. But the turnaround, which did happen eventually, took some more time. He sent out numerous letters to well-wishers to secure a job that would be to his liking and would also pay a satisfactory salary, but those attempts came out a cropper. He was keen on a desk job where he could apply his intellect as well as his good command over the English language, a skill rather scarce in Mewar in those days. But the only offer that came his way was for a primary schoolteacher, which did not interest him. That was the job many students in Banera who could not go beyond middle school eventually did. Father was looking for something more challenging.

At the same time, given his financial condition and the responsibility of a family that he had, he needed to find something that would pay a decent salary. Therefore, when a rich but distant relative offered him a job in a cloth shop manned by his son in

Ajmer, he accepted it. Assuming that the relative would offer him a fair deal, and thinking that it would be impolite to ask him what salary he would be paid, he did not ask anything about the job. He went off to Ajmer and began working at the shop. A week into the job, he finally decided to ask his relative's son the terms of his employment. He was told he would be paid Rs 10 per month. That was well below my father's expectation. Therefore, he immediately quit the job and left Ajmer.

From Ajmer, Father came to Udaipur and once again began searching for a job, possibly with the princely state of Mewar. Luckily, the warden at Jain Hostel was fond of him and let him stay free of charge. Given my father's meagre financial resources, this was a big help. After some inquiries, Father found out that the office of the accountant general had a vacancy for a clerk with a command over the English language. This was clearly the kind of job he wanted, so he approached the accountant general. Unfortunately, the accountant general not only lacked the qualifications for his own job, he was also rude and arrogant. When Father finally got an audience with him and enquired about the position, the accountant general denied that such a vacancy existed in his office. Disappointed, Father left the office, only to learn later that the accountant general had lied to him and had had the vacancy filled by someone else.

Father was now experiencing first-hand what nepotism and patronage, practised by the Mewar government, did to ordinary citizens who had the qualifications for employment but lacked family connections. But he soon got indirect help from an unlikely quarter. The British government had recently forced the Maharana to replace an uneducated feudal lord with a retired district judge from United Provinces as the Chief Justice of the Chief Court.

The Chief Court and its subordinate courts did not have a single employee with even workable knowledge of English. Therefore, when my father approached this Chief Justice, who owed nothing to the Maharana, he advised him to work in his office pro bono till a vacancy opened.

My father saw this as a lifeline of sorts and began working with the Chief Justice. He prepared summaries of the files at the court, positively impressing the Chief Justice with his skills. But, uncertain about how long it might take for a vacancy to open up at the court, he also kept exploring other job opportunities on the side. He soon landed an offer to work with a well-known historian in Ajmer. Because the prospects of a paid position in the Chief Court remained uncertain and he felt embarrassed about living in Jain Hostel free of charge for an entire month, he decided to accept the offer. He went to the Chief Justice and explained to him his predicament. The Chief Justice understood, and immediately relieved him of his duties, but told him to leave his home address with the peshkar (court clerk) before leaving office.

Bhilwara was on the way to Ajmer from Udaipur, so Father thought that he would make use of the opportunity to visit home in Suwana. After spending a couple of days there, he was ready to leave for Ajmer. Because he planned to take an early morning train to Ajmer from Bhilwara, he decided to spend the day before the journey at a hostel in Bhilwara. At the hostel, he happened to meet a gentleman who had just been transferred to Bhilwara to serve as a reader in the office of the hakim. As luck would have it, Father missed the train to Ajmer the next morning and had to return to the hostel. His next option was a train to Ajmer at 5.30 p.m. An hour before he was to leave for the railway station, however, the gentleman he had met the previous evening came looking for him. He told him that the hakim had received orders from the Chief Justice in Udaipur appointing my father as the ahalmad (clerk) in the court of the naib hakim in Mandal, a tehsil in Bhilwara district. Father went immediately to see the hakim, who refused to even look at him. After waiting for half an hour, when my father decided to give up and got up to leave, the hakim curtly told him to go and take up the position in Mandal.

At last, my father's search for a suitable job had a happy ending. Next morning, on 15 August 1938, he left for Mandal instead of Ajmer and took charge of his job. He was only seventeen years old at the time and had to fill the shoes of a middle-aged man with twenty-five years of experience. He knew nothing about the job, which led the naib hakim to complain to the Chief Justice in Udaipur. Having observed him first-hand during the few days that he had worked in his office, the Chief Justice was confident that my father had it in him to do the job. He wrote back to the naib hakim that it was his duty to train the young man. That was the end of the matter.

I may narrate here an incident that illustrates graphically how degenerate the system of justice in the state of Mewar had become around this time. Soon after my father joined as a clerk in Mandal, a hakim was appointed in Bhilwara. He replaced the man who had received the order from the Chief Justice appointing my father as a clerk in Mandal. Both he and his predecessor had limited schooling and lacked qualifications for the job. But they had the blessings of the Maharana. This new hakim was, additionally, a thoroughly corrupt man. He would not let go of any opportunity to amass personal wealth and would use the power of his office without hesitation towards this end.

On one occasion, the hakim got an individual arrested when the latter was in the midst of the twelve-day period of mourning following his mother's death. The accusation levelled against the accused was that in the letters he had sent to his friends and relatives informing them of the death of his mother, he had stated that she had left for 'deolok' (heaven). The hakim contended that only the Maharana and his courtiers were entitled to the use of the term 'deolok' when describing the death of a family member. He did not release the man until he had coughed up fifty rupees, a rather hefty sum for an ordinary citizen in those days. Luckily, real justice was served two years later, when T. Vijayaraghavacharya, appointed as the prime minister by the Maharana under pressure from the British, dismissed the hakim along with half a dozen other senior officials of doubtful integrity.

The naib hakim of Mandal was a law graduate and a sincere, honest and hardworking man. But being unconnected to the Maharana, he too became the object of harassment by the hakim of Bhilwara soon after the latter was appointed. The naib hakim requested the Mewar government to transfer him out of Bhilwara. The government granted the request and my father had another boss. This one had the blessings of the Maharana. Therefore, he was immune to harassment by the hakim.

By this time, my father had learned his job well. Taking advantage of this fact, the new happy-go-lucky naib hakim left the administration of the court entirely to him. That gave my father the opportunity to run the affairs of the court, ranging from taking down statements to keeping records to writing judgments. He got to deal with all aspects of civil as well as criminal cases. He enjoyed the work immensely and got an opportunity to read books on law so that he could take well-informed decisions. His experience and his reading came in handy later on, when he decided to do a degree in law.

The following three or four years saw my father grow professionally, with promotions coming his way, though with frequent transfers from one town to another. He had scarcely completed a year in Mandal when he was promoted to the position of nazir and sent to the District Court of Rajnagar, later renamed Rajsamand after the beautiful lake of the same name. Then, in October 1940, he was appointed as reader in the court of a magistrate in Kapasan. After another three months, in January 1941, he moved to Bhilwara as reader in the court of the first-class magistrate there. That too lasted only five months, and he was moved to Chittor.

In the meantime, in January 1941, my father's first child, my oldest sister, Premlata, arrived even before he had reached twenty years of age. This was not unusual in those days. His own father had had his first child at an even younger age. In the following eleven years, my parents would have another five children, of whom all but one would survive and would go on to lead rich lives. Only the second child, a boy born in November 1942, would die of pneumonia at the tender age of ten months. I would be the last of their six children, arriving in 1952. The first two of my siblings would be sisters and the next two brothers. With a gap of just two years between the successive boys, we three brothers would grow up with a great sense of camaraderie.

The first year of my father's appointment in the Mewar government, 1938, had coincided with the formation of the Mewar Praja Mandal. Keen on joining the freedom movement when the opportunity came, he closely followed its activities. Upon its formation, the organization launched a movement for the establishment of a responsible government in the state. That led the Mewar government to immediately ban it and exile its leader, Manikya Lal Verma. It also went on to arrest the workers of the Praja Mandal in the major towns, such as Udaipur, Bhilwara, Chittor and Nathdwara. My father was in Mandal at the time and had maintained close contact with the local workers of the organization. Clandestinely, he would even get banned weekly newspapers from Ajmer. The newspapers carried information on the arrests that had been happening in the various towns of Mewar.

When T. Vijayaraghavacharya became the prime minister of Mewar in 1939, he decided to lift the ban on the Praja Mandal and freed all political prisoners. Soon after, in 1940, at my father's request, Mewar Praja Mandal President Verma visited Suwana. He interacted closely with the village folk and exhorted them to join the Mewar Praja Mandal. A special relationship developed between him and the village, with the result that he maintained close contact with it till his death in 1969. The villagers, of course, adored him. My father and a number of his friends became his lifelong fans. Later, my father founded a branch of the Mewar Praja Mandal in Suwana with himself as its president.

After the release of its members from jail, the Mewar Praja Mandal resumed its activities, which culminated in its first formal session in Udaipur in 1941. Verma presided over the session. Vijaya Laxmi Pandit, the sister of Jawaharlal Nehru, gave the open inaugural address, which attracted thousands of people.

At the time of the session, my father was posted in Chittor. He came to know that the train on which Vijaya Laxmi Pandit was travelling to Udaipur would pass through Chittor and make a stop there in the early hours of morning. Keen to see someone so closely associated with the freedom movement in person, my father arrived at the station with a few of his friends at 4 a.m. As soon as the train came to a stop, he and his friends shouted repeatedly the slogan: '*Mahatma Gandhi ki jai!*'

Despite it being very early in the morning, Vijaya Laxmi Pandit came out of her compartment with a smile on her face and thanked the group for coming to see her at the station. The group offered her tea, which she graciously accepted. Within minutes, other passengers found out about her presence and quickly gathered around her. She gave a short speech on the struggle against the British that loomed ahead. Once the speech was over, the railway staff pleaded with the passengers to return to their respective compartments. The train then left amid cries of '*Vijaya Laxmi Pandit ki jai!*' At twenty years of age, seeing a figure so intimately linked with the freedom movement of India was a great source of inspiration for my father.

Meanwhile, the Second World War had begun in September 1939 on the world stage. Without consultations with the local leadership, the British had unilaterally announced India's involvement in it. That did not go down well with the Congress, which immediately responded by resigning from the provincial governments it headed. Later, as the pressures of the war mounted and the Japanese army began advancing towards India through Burma, the British realized that they needed India's military cooperation and the support of its political leadership.

Accordingly, in March 1942, they sent a Commission under Stafford Cripps with the offer of dominion status for India upon the end of the war in exchange for military cooperation. But to appease Muslim nationalism and princely aspirations, the offer left the door open for eventual secession of some provinces and princely states from the dominion. Describing the offer as a post-dated cheque written on a failed bank, Mahatma Gandhi rejected it and, on 8 August 1942, decided to launch the Quit India movement. He called upon all Indians to 'do or die' in the cause of the country's freedom. The next day, all the leaders of the Congress and Gandhi himself were arrested. It was time for all Indians to rise against the alien power.

By this time, my father had been promoted and transferred from Chittor back to Bhilwara as reader in the Court of the District and Sessions Judge. He had been residing in Suwana and commuted daily to the court in Bhilwara. Here I briefly digress to narrate an incident that throws light on an interesting aspect of life in Mewar in those days.

One evening, when my father was returning from Bhilwara to Suwana by bullock cart, a gang of dacoits stopped him and his co-passengers, numbering about half a dozen. At sword-point, the gang robbed them of everything they had, including their clothes. Just as the gang was about to go away, its leader saw Father and his co-passengers shivering in the cold. He took pity on them and returned some of their clothes. Paradoxically, the robbed ended up thanking the robbers profusely for their generosity!

Father and his co-passengers decided not to report the matter to the police for fear that the gang might take revenge on them. Six months passed and they forgot all about the incident. Then, one day, Father suddenly saw the gang in the Sessions Court where he was working as a reader. Apparently, its members had been arrested and committed to the court on charges of murder and dacoity. They saw my father and recognized him. They then narrated the entire incident of how they had first robbed him and his co-passengers of everything and then had returned their clothes to save them from the severe cold. It was a story that gave the members of the bar, the judge and the entire staff a hearty laugh.

To return to the main story, soon after the arrest of Mahatma Gandhi, the top leaders of Mewar Praja Mandal were also arrested. At this juncture, my father and two of his friends from Suwana felt that they too wanted to become full participants in the freedom movement and offer themselves for arrest. They immediately communicated their wish to the district-level leadership of the Praja Mandal in Bhilwara. The latter advised my father and his friends to wait for a signal from them.

While they awaited the signal, Bhanwarlal Bhadada, a prominent worker of the Praja Mandal in Bhilwara, visited Suwana. Later, he would become a close personal friend of my father and would often visit us in Jaipur. We would come to know him as 'Dada Bhai'. On his visit to Suwana, Dada Bhai brought my father and his friends the disappointing news that the Congress had now decided against Praja Mandal workers courting further arrest. Instead, it wanted them to engage in constructive social work. As a result, neither Dada Bhai nor my father and his friends got to court arrest.

My father was deeply disappointed that a chance to be an active participant in the national movement had been missed. Because this would turn out to be his first and last such chance, he would later write in his autobiography, 'An opportunity to contribute our bit in the final battle for swaraj had been lost! I still regret it.'[6] But all was not lost. The departure of the British would not spell full freedom for the citizens of princely states such as Mewar. That would require a separate, final battle against the Maharajas and

6 Panagariya, *My Little World.*

Maharanas. My father would be able to substantively contribute to that battle.

As part of the mandate for constructive social work by Mahatma Gandhi, the following year, my father played a key role in piloting the opening of a model school in Suwana. The proposal for the school came from Dada Bhai on behalf of the Praja Mandal, and funding came from an industrial house in Bhilwara. Called Gram Vidyalaya (village school), the school came to life in July 1943 and served the children from Suwana and nearby villages till the early 1970s, when it was closed down to make way for a high school.

In addition to serving as an institution of learning, the school became a focal point of social and cultural gatherings in the village. In September 1944, it brought such literary figures of India as Makhan Lal Chaturvedi and Ramnath 'Suman' to Suwana. The same year, Manikya Lal Verma visited the school. His daughter, young student leader Shiv Charan Mathur, and Kamal Nayan Bajaj, son of the late Jamnalal Bajaj, accompanied him. It was during this visit that Verma announced the engagement of his daughter and Shiv Charan Mathur. Later, in the first half of the 1980s, Mathur went on to become the chief minister of the state of Rajasthan. In 1968, as the serving education minister of the state, he visited my school as the chief guest at the annual function, where I received a prize from him for my exceptional performance in the secondary school examinations. I distinctly remember him asking me if I was the son of B.L. Panagariya. My father and he had worked together in the Verma government of the United State of Rajasthan and had come to know each other well.

My father stayed in his job in Bhilwara until August 1946. During this period, he remained actively engaged with the affairs of the school in Suwana and even taught night classes in general knowledge and English. It was perhaps because of this teaching experience that when my brothers and I were growing up, he would conduct a general knowledge quiz for us in the evenings as we gathered around him. He was also quick to correct our English, especially our pronunciation. Since we had all studied in a Hindi-medium school, our English required such correction rather frequently.

At work, Father also fought for the rights of his fellow employees. One fight concerned the salaries of court employees. Bhilwara had been known for its textiles industry. Its first modern unit, known as Mewar Textile Mills, started as far back as 1938. Soon after the end of the Second World War, workers of this mill threatened to go on strike unless the mill increased their wages to compensate for war-time inflation. The threat led Prime Minister T. Vijayaraghavacharya to intervene and get the mill owners to agree to a substantial increase in wages.

The success of the workers led my father to reason with his colleagues at the Sessions Court and its subordinate courts that wartime inflation had impacted their salaries to the same extent as it had the wages of the mill workers. His colleagues concurred. My father then prepared a memorandum making a case for increase in salary for the court staff and sent a copy, duly signed by his colleagues and himself, to the prime minister of Mewar in Udaipur. Much to his surprise, the prime minister bought his argument and granted them a salary increase of 12.5 per cent.

Udaipur hosted the three-day annual session, starting on 31 December 1945, of the All India States Peoples' Conference (AISPC), under the presidency of Jawaharlal Nehru. The conference brought together the leaders of the Praja Mandals and other popular organizations in the princely states from across the entire country. Among the prominent leaders who attended the conference were Sheikh Abdullah, a future chief minister of Jammu and Kashmir; Balwant Rai Mehta, the second chief minister of Gujarat; and Jai Narayan Vyas, the second chief minister of Rajasthan. Manikya Lal Verma, who led Mewar Praja Mandal, chaired the reception committee.

My father attended the proceedings of the AISPC and found them fascinating. The speeches by Nehru and Abdullah were the most impactful. Employees of the Mewar government chose to come to the sessions rather than attend to their duties in offices. The city of Udaipur came to a standstill during those three days. My father later wrote, 'The session brought new awakening amongst the people of the State.'[7] During the session, Manikya Lal Verma's daughter and Shiv Charan Mathur were married at a ceremony over which Jawaharlal Nehru presided. My father was among the few who attended the wedding.

Around this time, the employees of the Mewar government began to get organized to press the government for a pay increase and for reinstatement of two colleagues who had been suspended because they had been absent during the AISPC session. They formed a union, Mewar Ahalkar Sangh, and gave an ultimatum of strike if their demands were not met by 18 April 1946. The government acted preemptively and arrested the union leaders on 12 April 1946. That led to what turned out to be the first mass strike by government employees in the history of India. Resorting to the civil disobedience tactics of Mahatma Gandhi, the employees stopped going to work and began courting arrest every day. My father was the leader of the Bhilwara district branch of the union. The local collector threatened him in various ways, though he stopped short of arresting him.

---

7 B.L. Panagariya, *My Little World*.

At this point, my father approached Manikya Lal Verma, Bhure Lal Baya – who was then the president of Mewar Praja Mandal – and Ramesh Chandra Vyas, who was a leading Congress figure in the labour movement. He apprised them of the repression let loose on the employees by the Mewar government and sought their intervention. Verma immediately dispatched Vyas to Delhi to seek guidance from Nehru. Nehru in turn sent a note to the Mewar government condemning its high-handed actions against the poorly paid employees. That got the attention of the government.

The state government released the arrested employees, with no questions asked about their absence from work. It also set up a high-level committee to recommend new pay scales for different categories of employees. The final result was a significant upward revision of salaries for employees at all levels.

4

The Fall of the Ancient Régime of Mewar

THOUGH HE MISSED THE opportunity to be arrested as a part of the Quit India movement, my father remained keen on contributing to the freedom struggle in some capacity. As the employees' strike against the Mewar government came to a happy conclusion, he made up his mind to quit his job and join the Praja Mandal movement. His friends and relatives leaned heavily against his letting go of a 'secure and respectable' job, but his mind was made up.

This time around, he was not disappointed, and an opportunity came his way almost instantly. In August 1946, Siddharaj Dhadda, editor of a newly launched daily newspaper called *Lokvani* (People's Voice), visited Dada Bhai, the leader of the Praja Mandal in Bhilwara. Published from Jaipur, *Lokvani* had been originally started as a weekly in 1943. My father met Dhadda at Dada Bhai's residence. After listening to my father's aspirations of contributing to the freedom movement, Dhadda urged him to join *Lokvani*. He reasoned that the objectives of the newspaper being to support the activities of the Praja Mandals, raise a voice against the excesses of the feudal lords and promote the rights of peasants, my father would be able to fulfil his aspirations by working for it. Father instantly agreed to join *Lokvani*. His friends and relatives remained unequivocally opposed to the move, since it risked his losing a secure job. Therefore, as a compromise, he decided to take six months of leave without pay rather than resign his position outright.

The die was cast, and at twenty-five years of age, Father arrived in Jaipur for the first time on 19 September 1946. He found the city just as Rudyard Kipling had described it in his *Letters of Marque*. Hardly anything seemed to have changed in nearly fifty years since. During his travels of Rajputana, Kipling had passed through Jaipur at an even younger age of twenty-two. He had written engagingly about his travels. His write-ups first appeared anonymously in the newspaper *Allahabad Pioneer* between December 1887 and February 1888. Later, he brought those writings together in an authored volume.

As Kipling had described it, Jaipur was a well-planned city with wide roads intersecting at right angles. Picturesque buildings painted in pink adorned both sides of the city roads. The city was peaceful, with little traffic except in Johri Bazar, the hub of business activity. As my father would later recall, there were no cars or trucks on the roads back then, just a few cycle rickshaws.

Father had no prior experience of editing a newspaper. Though he found himself on a steep learning curve, he was soon in control of his duties at the editorial desk. Once he set up his routine, he was able to find the spare time to take up some writing of his own. He began publishing articles in *Lokvani,* and was soon pleasantly surprised that other newspapers were reproducing some of them. Given his deep knowledge of and interest in Mewar, many of his articles focused on its government and the activities of Mewar Praja Mandal.

One of my father's articles, entitled 'Seven Years of Sir T. Vijay in Mewar' contained a highly critical commentary on the policies of the Mewar government. It created a stir and left the Mewar government furious. In view of the fact that T. Vijayaraghavacharya, had been appointed at the instance of the British agent, the article must have annoyed the British government as well. The Mewar government instituted an inquiry into the affair, and finding out that the author of the article was none other than one of its own employees on a six-month sabbatical, proceeded to immediately terminate his services. That finally and formally ended Father's tenure with the Mewar government. It was hardly unexpected. Father knew all along that this would happen; the only issue was when and on what grounds. In any case, the controversy created by the article brought him what he thought was a bigger prize: the well-known nationalist English newspaper *Bombay Chronicle* appointed him as their accredited correspondent in Jaipur on a part-time basis while he continued to work at *Lokvani.*

With India rapidly moving towards independence from the British, this was a critical period in the nation's history. In September 1946, Nehru had formed the interim government at the Centre. Provinces directly under the British had formed governments responsible to elected legislatures. People in the princely states were also clamouring for the removal of hereditary kings and the appointment of popularly elected governments. Luckily for my father, the office of the Rajputana Regional Council of the AISPC was located in Jaipur. That brought the leaders of the Praja Mandals and Praja Parishads of Rajputana to Jaipur and gave my father the opportunity to establish close contact with them. These leaders would serve in top positions in the governments that were formed after unification of the Rajputana states into Rajasthan.

One immediate outcome of these contacts was that the Rajputana Regional Council of the AISPC asked my father to head a committee to inquire into allegations of oppression let loose by the Bharatpur government. Apparently, the Maharaja of Bharatpur had invited Viceroy Lord Wavell to his state for a game of bird hunting in the Keoladeo Bird Sanctuary (renamed Keoladeo National Park in 1982 and listed as a World Heritage Site by UNESCO in 1985). It was alleged that during the game, government authorities forced individuals from the Dalit community to recover the birds shot by the hunting party from the cold water of the lake in the sanctuary. That led the Bharatpur Praja Parishad and other peoples' organizations in the area to organize protests against such forced labour. The protests resulted in injuries to people as well as arrests by the Bharatpur government.

Because the protests were on account of a hunting game in which the Viceroy had been involved, Nehru asked his private secretary Dwarkanath Kachru to join the inquiry. My father and Kachru met the prime minster of Bharatpur and the arrested workers to get the stories on both sides and went on to submit the resulting report to the general secretary of the Rajputana Regional Council of the AISPC. Based on the report, the provincial leaders successfully resolved the matter with the Bharatpur government. Not only were the workers released from jail, the government agreed to democratization of the administration and to soon hold elections for a legislative assembly. Bharatpur thus moved one step closer to having people's rule established.

In March 1947, five months before Independence, the Mewar Praja Mandal held its annual session in Bijolia, a major town of great historical significance in Mewar state. My father attended the session, which offered him the opportunity to renew contacts with Manikya Lal Verma, Bhure Lal Baya – then president of Mewar Praja Mandal – and other leaders of the organization. The leaders thanked my father for the prominence his articles and other stories in *Lokvani* had been giving to the activities of the Praja Mandal. They then requested him to start a weekly paper from Udaipur on behalf of the Mandal. My father was reluctant, because Udaipur already had two other dailies. Therefore, no decision could be taken on the paper and he returned to Jaipur.

The situation changed two months later, however. In May 1947, the Maharana of Mewar, Bhupal Singh, adopted a new constitution framed by K. M. Munshi, under which he agreed to hold state assembly elections. He also agreed to include two nominees of the Praja Mandal in his cabinet in the interim. With elections now on the anvil, the Praja Mandal leadership decided that it must have a weekly paper to carry its message to the people.

In July 1947, Verma and Mohan Lal Sukhadia, who later went on to become the longest-serving chief minister of Rajasthan, came to Jaipur for business at the office of the Rajputana Regional Council of the AISPC. They visited my father at his home and urged him to take charge of the proposed weekly. With the context having changed due to the impending elections, my father now saw an opportunity in the proposed newspaper. It could potentially influence the election outcome in favour of Mewar Praja Mandal. Accordingly, he accepted the proposal. Dhadda, the editor of *Lokvani*, readily relieved him of his duties at the newspaper.

My father wrapped up his affairs in Jaipur to move to Udaipur. Bhilwara happens to be on the way to Udaipur from Jaipur. Being aware that India was set to win its independence from the British on 15 August 1947, he decided to take the opportunity to be in Suwana on the great day before proceeding to Udaipur. He thought this would be a good opportunity to organize a celebration of India's Independence with fellow villagers. With the birth of my second sister Kamala on 2 June 1945, his family now included my mother and two daughters. Together, they travelled first to Bhilwara and thence to Suwana.

Like the rest of the country, citizens of Suwana were hugely excited about India's independence on 15 August. Led by my father, they organized a function at which the national flag was unfurled, speeches were given and the national anthem sung. The function ended with the slogans '*Mahatma Gandhi ki jai*' and '*Pandit Nehru ki jai*'. Later, the villagers constructed a platform on the spot from which speeches had been delivered that day. They named it 'Azad Platform'.

During the celebrations, my father found that some of the villagers remained unconvinced that freedom from the British had actually been achieved. If the British had really quit India, how come the rupee coin still carried the figure of the British king, they asked sceptically. My father patiently explained that it would take some time before new coins were minted to replace the old ones. If the old coins were withdrawn even before new coins had been minted and put into circulation, people would face immense hardship in buying and selling goods and services. That seemed to satisfy the villagers.

After spending a little longer than a month in Suwana, Father left for Udaipur on 15 September 1947. My mother, who was expecting my oldest brother at the time, stayed back with the two daughters in Suwana. By the time Father arrived in Udaipur, the Praja Mandal had made all logistical arrangements for publication of the proposed weekly. An office of the newspaper had been set up. A founder-member of the Praja Mandal, who owned a press in Udaipur, had agreed to print the weekly free of charge. Freedom fighter Amritlal Sheth, founder-editor of the Gujarat daily *Janmabhoomi*, which continues to publish even today, had agreed to provide newsprint. Patriotic Praja Mandal workers, some of whom later became legislators and ministers, offered to serve as hawkers to distribute the weekly. The working committee of Mewar Praja Mandal formally named the weekly *Mewar Praja Mandal Patrika* and appointed my father as its editor.

The first issue of the weekly was published on 2 October 1947, the last birth anniversary of Mahatma Gandhi before he was assassinated. The paper quickly became popular and acquired a readership of 2,500, which was an impressive figure, given the tiny proportion of the population that read newspapers in those days and the prior existence of two well-established dailies in the town. Editors of both existing newspapers, who had initially resented the Praja Mandal's starting a paper of its own, congratulated my father for the high-quality content and the design of the weekly.

The weekly highlighted the activities of the Praja Mandal and informed people all over Mewar what it would do when it came to power. It explained the significance of the first-ever elections to the state assembly. It relentlessly exposed the excesses of the feudal system and thus laid the groundwork for the abolition of jagirs and jagirdars upon the establishment of a Praja-Mandal-led popular government. It leaned heavily against the merger of the states of Rajputana into neighbouring states and championed the cause of integration of all the Rajputana states into one, which eventually did come about in the form of the state of Rajasthan.

Though the process of assembly elections began in February 1948, actual voting was to take place in the first half of April 1948. Pending formation of the assembly, under pressure from the states department of the central government, the Maharana agreed to constitute a representative interim government consisting of seven members, with four of them coming from the Praja Mandal. One of the four Praja Mandal members was to head the government as the prime minister. Kshatriya Parishad, which essentially represented the interests of the feudal lords in the state, was to appoint two members. The remaining member was to be an independent person acceptable to both the Maharana and the Praja Mandal. The Praja Mandal proposed Manikya Lal Verma as its nominee for the position of prime minister and three others as members. Kshatriya Parishad also proposed the names of two nominees from its side.

Sharp differences arose between the Maharana and the Praja Mandal, however, over the choice of the independent member. The Maharana proposed the name of Mohan Singh Mehta, the younger brother of Tej Singh Mehta, who had helped my father pay his fee for his high school examinations. Mohan Singh Mehta now served as the finance minister in the government of the Maharana and enjoyed his confidence. Unfortunately, he was persona non grata with the Praja Mandal since 1942, when, as the education minister, he had attempted to break a student strike in support of the Quit India movement. Even in the recent past, his relations with the Praja Mandal had been less than cordial. The Praja Mandal therefore opposed Mehta and suggested an alternative candidate. Given that the states department was with the Praja Mandal, the Maharana had no choice but to acquiesce. The episode left a bad taste in the mouth for him.

To complete the rest of the story, it is necessary to briefly digress towards the process of integration of the princely states of Rajputana into the Union of India, which was underway full steam at this time. By early 1948, the states department of the central government had adopted a policy whereby small princely states that did not constitute viable administrative units on their own would be merged either into neighbouring provinces or with other princely states to create a larger, viable unit. Princely states that were large enough to be viable administrative units on their own were allowed to keep their independent identity.

Following these principles, in early 1948, the states department integrated nine smaller states and two chiefships in southern and southeastern Rajputana into a single unit, christened United State of Rajasthan (USR). A problem with USR, however, was that although its component states shared a common language and culture, they lacked geographical contiguity. The only way to achieve contiguity was to either merge the USR states into Mewar or to get the latter to accede to the former. But neither alternative was available: the component states of USR did not want that a larger neighbour should gobble them up, and Mewar State did not want to lose its identity by acceding to the USR. The states department was keen on one of these alternatives, but its hands were tied. Having been in existence for more than a millennium,

Mewar had demonstrated that it was a viable administrative unit and amply qualified to remain an independent state.

As mentioned earlier, the Praja Mandal had antagonized the Maharana on the question of the inclusion of Mehta in the interim cabinet. Mehta and another minister in the outgoing cabinet exploited this situation by telling the Maharana that if the Praja Mandal came to power it might not deliver many of the privileges to which he was entitled under the policy of the states department. On the other hand, if he now offered to merge Mewar into USR, the states department might reward him with a much larger package.

The Maharana was persuaded to their point of view, and he informed the states department on 23 March 1948 that he was willing to join USR, provided he were given two million rupees instead of the standard one million rupees annually in Privy Purse, he and his descendants were granted the position of rajpramukh (equivalent to governor in the previously British-ruled provinces) in perpetuity, and Udaipur was made the capital of greater USR. For the states department, this was too big a prize to pass up. It agreed to the conditions, with one exception: it granted the position of rajpramukh to the Maharana for life but not to his descendants. To get around its cap of one million rupees on the Privy Purse, it gave the Maharana half a million rupees in salary as rajpramukh and another half a million rupees for charitable and religious purposes.

On 11 April 1948, the states department got the rulers of Mewar and other component states of USR to sign the covenant. In the meantime, the Maharana and the others involved kept the matter secret so that the Praja Mandal leaders remained oblivious to the development. The Maharana also managed to delay the swearing-in of the interim government on one pretext or the other. The fact that the Praja Mandal was preoccupied with the elections to the legislative assembly made it easier for the Maharana to accomplish both objectives.

Immediately after the rulers signed the covenant acceding to USR, the states department informed the Mewar Praja Mandal of the development by telephone. At the time, the Praja Mandal had been engaged in a life-and-death struggle in the assembly elections against the feudal powers that had come to unite in their opposition to it. Aided by the Maharana, the latter stood a decent chance of victory. Therefore, the Praja Mandal leadership received the news of the acquiescence of the Maharana to Mewar's accession to USR with great relief. More importantly, the accession effectively accomplished for the Praja Mandal the purpose for which it had been created. A defeat in the elections, which could not have been ruled out, would have left the feudal lords still in power. But Mewar's accession to USR wiped out that possibility. A regime that had ruled Mewar for more than a millennium had finally fallen and paved the way for emergence of people's rule. What the Praja Mandal had failed to do, the mutsaddi had accomplished for it!

The states department nominated popular leader Manikya Lal Verma as the prime minister of the newly formed USR. It then went on to advise Verma that since he and his associates lacked administrative experience, it would appoint an executive council consisting of the outgoing prime minister of Mewar, the outgoing finance minister, Mehta, and the regional commissioner of Rajputana. The department told Verma that in case of a difference of opinion between the cabinet and the executive council, a reference would be made to the states department, whose decision would be final.

Verma had fought all his life to establish people's rule in Mewar and had no intention to head a government that would be under effective control of the same retrograde clique that had guided the Maharana. Therefore, he refused to accept the arrangement. He met Sardar Vallabhbhai Patel, the minister in charge of the states department, and told him that rather than head a government whose decisions were subject to veto by bureaucrats, the Praja Mandal and he would prefer to serve the people from outside. Patel got the message and dropped the proposal for the advisory council.

On 18 April 1948, Nehru came to Udaipur and inaugurated the new United State of Rajasthan. The Maharana took the oath of office of the rajpramukh and Verma of the office of prime minister. Six others, including Bhure Lal Baya, were sworn in as ministers in the cabinet. My father was proud to have witnessed the historic event first-hand.

The objective of *Mewar Praja Mandal Patrika* accomplished, a decision was made to close it down. My father's experience at helming the periodical had been hugely rewarding. He had been able to actively participate in the last leg of the journey of the Praja Mandal to 'free' the state of Mewar from the long rule of hereditary rulers for more than a millennium. He got to observe, from a ringside seat, a critical step towards the formation of what would come to be known as the state of Rajasthan. Years later, after retirement, he would take to writing yet again and would be able to give an eyewitness account of the formation of the United State of Rajasthan in his book *Rajasthan Mein Swatantra Sangram.* The book would become the standard and, indeed, the only original reference of its kind on the history of the freedom movement in Rajasthan.

Anticipating the closure of *Mewar Praja Mandal Patrika*, Father had been planning to return to *Lokvani* in Jaipur and resume working with the Congress. Therefore, when Siddharaj Dhadda, the editor of the newspaper, came to Udaipur on the occasion of the inauguration of the Unites State of Rajasthan, the two of them met Prime Minister Verma. Contrary to their expectation, Verma advised against the move, telling them that he wanted the services of my father for the new state.

Having no idea what Verma had in mind, my father decided to take a break for the time being and return to Suwana. He had devoted ten to twelve hours each day on the *Mewar Praja Mandal Patrika*, taking only two days off to visit Hurda in Bhilwara district, where my mother had given birth to Ravi on 24 January 1948. At the time, my mother's brother was posted in Hurda, and Ravi was born in his home. By now, my mother and the three children were back in Suwana. Therefore, Father could be in their company on his visit to Suwana before taking the next step of his professional life.

When Father arrived in Suwana, fellow villagers received him with great warmth and excitement. Once again, he had the opportunity to hold meetings with them on the grand platform outside the house. He told them stories of how the United State of Rajasthan had been formed, how Pandit Nehru had administered the oath of office to the Maharana and to Manikya Lal Verma, and how the popular leaders whom the totalitarian regime had jailed only a few years back were now ministers and governed the newly formed state.

Though he may not have realized it, my father's own story of the preceding fifteen years mirrored that of these leaders. Back in 1936, his mother had died a lonely death after the community Panchas had heaped insult after insult on her for nearly two years. Today, he enjoyed a commanding position in the village. To his credit, he never let the miseries and insults his mother had suffered come in the way of his love for the village. In the years that followed, he did not miss a single opportunity to bring the fruits of development to the village. Having become a part of the government at the founding of the state of Rajasthan, he successfully brought in road connectivity, Ayurvedic and allopathic dispensaries, a post office, a panchayat samiti, piped water, a veterinary outpost and the first high school.

5

In the Service of the People of Rajasthan

FATHER HAD SCARCELY GOT a few days of well-deserved rest when he received a telegram from Bhure Lal Baya, minister of jagirs in the newly formed USR, asking him to leave for Udaipur immediately. When he arrived in Udaipur and went to see Baya, the latter asked him to go and see Prime Minister Verma. Verma told him that he wanted to appoint some of the younger Praja Mandal workers to suitable positions in different departments of the secretariat. Evidently, he wanted political appointees to play a critical role in the running of his government. He also told my father that now that the Praja Mandal leadership was in charge of the government, it did not make a difference whether he worked for the government or for the Congress; the two amounted to one and the same thing. My father told him that his services were at his disposal and that he could make use of them as he saw fit.

The Verma government soon appointed a dozen Praja Mandal workers from the component states of USR to key positions. Among others, they included Shiv Charan Mathur and Niranjan Nath Acharya, who would later become leading politicians in the state of Rajasthan. My father was initially appointed as head of the Directorate of Publicity, but at his request was moved to the Department of Commerce and Industry as undersecretary. The minister in charge of the department was Mohan Lal Sukhadia.

Upon taking charge, my father discovered that the former rulers of the component states of USR had strangulated the process of industrialization. They would take many years to give permission to even small-scale units to be set up. Availability of electricity was limited, and what was available was used up in lighting the palaces of the rulers. In what was one of the earliest acts of liberalizing reforms in India's post-Independence history, my father suggested that when an entrepreneur was not seeking any assistance or concessions from the government, he should be given permission to set up industries freely and promptly. The secretary of the department expressed reservations, but the minister supported the proposal and the policy was implemented. That led to the establishment of a number of small industrial units almost immediately.

The Verma government in USR got to rule for only eleven months, because during this period the states department successfully merged all the princely states of Rajputana to form the present-day state of Rajasthan. But, as historians including my father have documented in detail, the Verma government accomplished in its eleven months more than what other governments subsequently did even in a full five-year term. The secretariat was set up and various departments established. The integration of services of as many as ten component states was completed within three months, to the satisfaction of all involved. Levies collected by jagirdars on various occasions, such as birth, marriage, death and festivals, were abolished. And, most importantly, the government put an effective end to the tyranny of the feudal lords. The weekly paper my father had edited had promised the people that if the Praja Mandal came to power, it would put an end to this repressive system. Verma successfully delivered on that.

When Verma went to Delhi to get the states department on board on the subject of ending the feudal system, the latter expressed concern that the step might create a law-and-order problem and undermine its ongoing efforts to unify the Rajputana states into a single state. Verma argued that the freedom movement and abolition of the princely order had greatly weakened the feudal lords, so this was the right time to strike. He personally assured Patel that he would carry out the entire operation peacefully without a single shot having to be fired. He returned to Udaipur only after Patel had blessed the project.

Upon his return, Verma issued two ordinances. The first transferred all revenue, executive and judicial powers from the jagirdars to the government. The second prohibited jagirdars from evicting tenants of any category from the land they tilled. With one exception, there was no resistance to the implementation of the two ordinances. In the solitary case of disturbance, police brought the situation under control within a few hours. For the millions of citizens of USR who had suffered the tyranny of jagirdars for centuries, Verma proved to be a true prophet.

During the eleven months that the Verma government ruled USR, the states department kept up the pressure on the remaining viable states – Jaipur, Jodhpur and Bikaner – to either merge into neighbouring provinces or with other Rajputana states to form a greater Rajasthan state. By early January 1949, all three states had been forced into submission. The states department granted two concessions to Maharaja Man Singh of Jaipur, namely, that Jaipur will be the capital of the new state and that he will be appointed its rajpramukh.

On 14 January 1949, Patel went to Udaipur with his daughter to convey the message to the USR government. My father was a member of the Verma-led delegation that received Patel. Later, at a public meeting in Sajjan Niwas garden in Udaipur, Patel announced that the rulers of Jaipur, Bikaner and Jodhpur had agreed to merge their states into Rajasthan.

On 30 March 1949, Patel inaugurated 'greater Rajasthan' in Jaipur, which became the capital of the state. Man Singh of Jaipur was appointed the rajpramukh, the Maharana of Mewar as the maharajpramukh and Hiralal Shastri, a prominent leader of the Jaipur Praja Mandal, as the chief minister. Verma chose to stay out of the government. Following Independence, members of the Praja Mandals in the princely states had been formally inducted into the Congress. Accordingly, Verma became an influential member of the Rajasthan Pradesh Congress Committee, playing the role of kingmaker in the following decade. He also served as a member of the lower house of Parliament.

Hiralal Shastri appointed Bhure Lal Baya to his cabinet. Baya, in turn, appointed my father as his private secretary. The two came together by plane from Udaipur to Jaipur on the morning of 7 April 1949, where Baya took his oath of office the same day.

After staying in a temporary accommodation for six weeks, my father was allotted a residence on the first floor of a house named Bhagwat Bhawan on Mirza Ismail Road, more commonly known by its abbreviated name, M.I. Road. This is the house in which my brother Ashok was born on 22 August 1950, and I on 2 October 1952. We lived in this house till 1957. I still have a clear memory of it. On a visit to Jaipur some years ago, I went to M.I. Road and found that structurally, the house looked hardly any different from outside than when we lived there. The only noticeable change was that the house looked a lot more run-down than during our days there. Hardly any effort seemed to have been made to give it a facelift.

In contrast to the house, M.I. Road had undergone a drastic change in look and feel since the days we lived there. From the veranda of our home on the first floor, we were able to observe the traffic on the road. I remember sitting there and counting the cars going in either direction at the age of four or five. It would take quite a while before the count would cross one hundred. Today, traffic congestion on the road is so severe that even under one-way traffic rule, it can move only at a snail's pace. For pedestrians, crossing the road from one side to the other is nothing less than an adventure.

Sometime in 1957, we left the house on M.I. Road to live in another rented house in nearby C-Scheme area. Then, in 1959, we moved to what became the 'permanent' residence of the family. Located on Moti Doongari Road, or M.D. Road for short, this is the house my father built. He named it 'Rajniketan' after his father's first name. Since 1959, members of the family staying in Jaipur have always lived in this house. My father and mother lived there till their passing away in 2006 and 2015, respectively. Currently, it is home to my two brothers, Ravi and Ashok, and their families, as also my sister Kamala, who chose to remain single.

Among all the decisions my father made in his life, the one to join the government of the state of Rajasthan would turn out to be the most unwise, and he would come to regret it. When he joined the Verma government of USR in 1948, he was still only twenty-seven years old and a rising star within the Mewar Praja Mandal. He stood a fair chance of emerging as one of the key figures among the second-generation of leaders of Rajasthan. But his rise would soon be capped within the bureaucracy of the new state. To be sure, he would remain highly influential, contributing handsomely to the betterment of the state and its people, but this would be largely due to his individual ability, determination and desire to work in the public interest rather than exult in the positions he would hold. Much greater personal success would come to him after his retirement, when he would launch an entirely new career as a writer and historian. In that incarnation, he would leave one of the best historical accounts of the contribution of Rajasthan to the national freedom movement and the post-Independence history of Rajasthan.

In contrast to my father, two of his contemporaries in the Mewar Praja Mandal, Shiv Charan Mathur and Niranjan Nath Acharya, who chose to resign their positions in the government after the dissolution of the Verma government and return to politics, later emerged as major figures in state politics. Both of them went on to serve as ministers in various state governments for many years. Mathur eventually rose all the way to the top to occupy the office of chief minister, and Acharya got to serve as speaker of the Rajasthan state legislative assembly.

Keen to keep tight control over the evolution of the state under the new administration, the states department of the central government appointed two Indian Civil Service (ICS) officers as advisers to the state government, and a third as chief secretary. No decisions by the chief minister, ministers or the cabinet could be implemented without the concurrence of the advisers. Unlike Verma, who was a man of conviction and therefore had refused to accept a similar constraint on his decision-making powers by the states department, Shastri was too weak, personally as well as politically, to resist it. He lacked the political support of the Rajasthan Pradesh Congress Committee (RPCC) and got its formal endorsement only under pressure from Patel. As such, he owed his position to Patel and could not say no to him or to the states department.

Shastri lasted one year and nine months as chief minister and ended his tenure in ignominy, with few notable accomplishments to his credit. At home, he lacked the support of the RPCC. Then, by September 1950, he also lost the support of Sardar Patel at the Centre. It so happened that in the elections for the president of the All India Congress Committee on 29 August 1950, the contest was between Purushottam Das Tandon and J.B. Kripalani, who were backed by Patel and Nehru, respectively. Shastri made the mistake of supporting Nehru's candidate. Not only did Nehru's candidate lose but Patel, infuriated by Shastri's support of him, decided to sack him. Though Patel himself died in December 1950 before implementing the decision, Nehru, who inherited the charge of the states department, remained committed to his decision and advised Shastri to resign his position immediately.

At this juncture, an astrologer advised Shastri that he would survive as chief minister provided he avoided submitting his resignation for a week. Taking the advice seriously, Shastri went into hiding. But that did not change his fortunes. The central government eventually tracked him down in Indore, where he was staying with a friend. It sent him a message asking him to either resign within twenty-four hours or face dismissal. Shastri complied, sending in his resignation on 5 January 1951.

In parallel, another astrologer story played out with my father's minister, Baya. While Shastri was in hiding, a gentleman brought an astrologer to Baya's house. The astrologer studied the minister's horoscope and proceeded to predict that he would soon be offered Sardar Patel's job in the central government. While my father, who was present at the scene, was amused, the minister fell for the prediction. He was convinced that Shastri would eventually come out on top and keep his position as chief minister. From there, he thought there could be a path to his ascendency to Patel's position. Pleased, he asked my father to offer the astrologer a suitable amount in baksheesh. Knowing that the minister was not especially liberal in money matters, my father offered the astrologer a sum of Rs 21. But that left the minister flustered. He immediately called his son to bring a sum of Rs 101 from his mother and give it to the astrologer. The astrologer blessed the minister and happily walked out with what was a handsome sum in those days, especially for making a prediction that had no chance of coming true.

Throughout Shastri's rule, it was the advisers and the chief secretary who effectively wielded power in the state. They showed a general disdain for the political class, including ministers and officers such as my father who had come from public life. Secretaries, brought in mostly from the Centre by the advisers, also took orders from the latter, ignoring their ministers.

Baya, for whom my father worked, was an independent-minded and assertive minister. Therefore, he inevitably came into conflict with the advisers and the chief secretary. Because the work of the secretariat was conducted in English and Baya lacked working knowledge of it, he relied on my father to study the files and brief him. Though all his decisions were his own, his reliance on my father for the briefs led the advisers and the chief secretary to conclude that my father was the one instructing and instigating him. The advisers therefore came to see my father as the 'villain of peace', and later penalized him for it.

Of course, being young and idealistic, perhaps my father did not help his own case either. Beginning in the mid 1940s, after he joined the Mewar Praja Mandal, he had taken to wearing a dhoti (loincloth), kurta and the famous Gandhi cap, all made of the khadi cloth that Mahatma Gandhi had encouraged. He continued that practice even after joining the government. A couple of his colleagues had been doing the same. This was noticed by one of the advisers, who sent the message that the dress, especially the Gandhi cap, was identified with a particular political party. Therefore, people like my father would be well advised to switch to politically neutral attire. My father and his colleagues ignored the message and continued to wear the cap and the rest of their khadi outfit. That could not have pleased the adviser.

The axe fell on my father when the advisers got down to the task of integrating the services of the covenanting states into the new set-up. Article XVI of the Covenant, signed by the princely states of Rajputana and the Government of India to create the state of Rajasthan, guaranteed 'the continuation in service of the members of the public services on conditions not less advantageous than those on which they were serving in the covenanting state concerned'. But the advisers entirely ignored this guarantee.

Rather than integrate the services, the advisers took recourse to open recruitment. They laid down neither the criteria for judging the suitability of candidates for the positions to be filled nor the rules for fixing inter-se seniority. The result was that tehsildars and secretariat officers with no field experience were appointed to the Rajasthan Administrative Service on the one hand, and well-qualified officers of covenanting states were left out on the other. Some stenographers, clerks and superintendents were appointed to the newly constituted Rajasthan Secretariat Services in preference to a number of assistant secretaries and undersecretaries of the covenanting states. In one case, a chief engineer of a covenanting unit was downgraded to the post of assistant engineer, while his own subordinates were appointed as executive engineer and superintending engineer.

Perhaps the most disconcerting feature of the integration from my father's viewpoint was that those who had been close to the former rulers of the covenanting states were placed in senior positions, regardless of their academic qualifications, experience or seniority. In contrast, those who had been active in or even sympathetic to the national movement were downgraded or outright rejected. Unsurprisingly, in an unusually personal note in his widely read 1988 book, *State Politics in India*, he wrote, 'All these things troubled me a lot. I came to the reluctant conclusion that my decision to continue in service was wrong, as it was right when I had joined it in the Former Rajasthan (USR). I had, however, no more will to resign and face wilderness. So I continued in Government service for another twenty-five years to witness the functioning of the Rajasthan Government from close quarters.'[8]

Though my father does not say anything further on the matter, I have no doubt that the key factor behind his lacking the will to resign and return to politics, as Mathur and Acharya had done earlier, was that he was now a father of four children. Their future very much depended on his choice between staying with the Government of Rajasthan and returning to politics. Since politics is a 24x7 profession, a return to it would surely have had an adverse impact on his ability to groom and nurture his children during their formative years. Most likely, we would have faired poorly in our lives, as did the children of most of my father's contemporaries in politics.

No contemporary of my father who chose politics can today boast of having fathered a son who distinguished himself in the private sector as an engineer, two children who were honoured with the Padma Shri and Padma Bhushan, and a daughter who won an award from the President of India for her services as a teacher. Though he did not live to celebrate these accomplishments, it can perhaps be said, in hindsight, that his decision to remain with the Government of Rajasthan was the right one after all!

During approximately four years following the exit of Hiralal Shastri on 5 January 1951, the office of chief minister changed hands as many times. Jay Narayan Vyas, the founder of Jodhpur Praja Mandal and later the prime minister of Jodhpur state, occupied the office for three of the four years over two separate stints. An ICS officer named C.S. Venkatachar, who served for three months immediately following Shastri and Tikaram Paliwal,

---

8 B.L. Panagariya, *State Politics in India*, Jaipur: National Publishing House, 1988, pp. 59-60

who served for nine months between the two terms of Vyas, filled the remaining year.

During these four years, my father served as private secretary to two ministers, Balwant Singh Mehta during the first term of Vyas, and Bholenath during his second term. In both cases, it was upon the insistence of the ministers that he agreed to join them. In the case of Mehta, a common friend came with the offer to my father's home. Father expressed serious reservations on the grounds that his former boss, Baya, had belonged to the opposite political camp of Mehta's. But the friend was unmoved, stating that the minister was convinced that my father was the right choice for the job. In the case of Bholenath, my father had not known him previously at all. But the minister was insistent on him.

Because both ministers had great respect for my father's knowledge, experience and judgement, they actively sought his advice on all important issues with which their ministries dealt. That gave my father a chance to effectively contribute to the betterment of the state. On the personal front, when working with Bholenath, he could resume his studies, taking evening classes at Maharaja College in Jaipur. He managed to complete both his BA and LLB degrees during this period. The knowledge of law he had acquired while working for the Mewar government and subsequently for USR and the state of Rajasthan came in handy in his study of law. He topped his LLB examination at the university and won high praise from the advocate general and the principal of the Law College of the time, Rai Bahadur S.K. Hajela. He was also awarded a gold medal for his performance, currently in possession of Ravi.

Remarkably, soon after my birth on 2 October 1952, my father got a vasectomy done. In this respect, he was well ahead of his time. In those days, few underwent the operation in a place like Jaipur. Indeed, Jaipur had no more than one or two doctors who performed it. Father had begun to appreciate the importance of family planning for India relatively early and took it upon himself to exert pressure on relatives and those working under him, who had two or three children already, to undergo a vasectomy.

In his first term, Vyas had the state Congress fully and firmly behind him. This was due in no small measure to the fact that he worked closely with the members of his cabinet and consulted the leadership of the RPCC on a regular basis. But when the first general elections took place in the country in March 1952, he lost his own seat in the legislative assembly. This led to the selection of his outgoing deputy chief minister, Tikaram Paliwal, as interim chief minister. The loss of his seat greatly weakened Vyas's hand vis-à-vis the RPCC leadership. To add to the problem, when he returned as chief minister the second time after winning a by-election in November 1952, his working style changed for the worse. He began relying heavily on his chief secretary, an ICS officer, to the neglect of his ministerial colleagues and other senior Congress party leaders, including the RPCC president and Verma. That, in the end, proved his undoing. Within a year, tensions between him and some members of his cabinet escalated to the point that he felt compelled to seek a vote of confidence within the Congress Legislative Party. The vote took place in November 1954, and much to his disappointment he lost to the rival group led by Mohan Lal Sukhadia.

On 13 November 1954, Sukhadia became the chief minister. He was a second-generation leader and the youngest chief minister in India at the time. He remained chief minister of Rajasthan for seventeen long years, till July 1971, when Prime Minister Indira

Gandhi unceremoniously removed him and sent him to Karnataka as governor. His mistake was that in the 1969 presidential election, which had pitched Gandhi against the organizational wing of the Indian National Congress, he had sided with the latter.

Like many of his cabinet colleagues, Bholenath too had disapproved of the working style of Vyas during his second term. But when the vote of confidence took place, he voted for Vyas because he considered him to be head and shoulders above Sukhadia as a leader. That, of course, meant that he was not included in the new cabinet, and my father became potentially available to serve with another minister. Sampatram, one of the members of the new cabinet, whom Father had known for some time, approached him with the offer to join him as his private secretary.

But at this juncture, my father felt that he had served as private secretary to ministers sufficiently long and it was time for him to begin serving as an officer in one of the departments in the secretariat. He conveyed this decision to the minister, but promised that he would fill the gap till he could find a suitable regular private secretary for him. He delivered on that promise within a couple of months and returned to the Government of Rajasthan as assistant secretary. He was initially posted in the appointments department for three months, but was moved to his regular position as assistant secretary, medical and health department, in March 1955.

Father served in the state of Rajasthan for another twenty-one years till his retirement on 30 June 1976, at the young age of fifty-five. During these years, he got only one promotion, to the post of deputy secretary, in February 1967. This was one step below the top bureaucratic position of secretary in those times. He did not reach the top position because all secretary-level positions were reserved for members of the Indian Administrative Services (IAS). He did try to transition into the IAS through selection, but luck turned out not to be on his side in this endeavour.

My father was selected for the Rajasthan Administrative Services (RAS) in May 1960, which offered a wider track to eventual selection in the IAS than the Rajasthan Secretariat Services (RSS), to which he belonged. But joining the RAS would have required moving from district to district in the course of his work and would have therefore interfered with his children's education. By this time, he knew that we were good at studies and had good prospects for future careers. Therefore, he chose to stay with the RSS, which guaranteed him location in Jaipur till retirement.

Given his exceptional performance, unmatched by any other officer of his rank, the state government recommended him for selection to the IAS on at least two occasions. But in the end, he lost out to rival candidates on both occasions. Each time my father knew in his heart of hearts, as did the selected candidate, that he was the superior candidate. But he never let the selected candidates feel that they had been given the prize that justly belonged to him. On the contrary, when one of the selected candidates came to see him the day after his selection was announced, Father received him with great warmth and profusely congratulated him. Ravi remembers to this day witnessing the event and feeling a sense of disappointment, knowing that the selected candidate, a veterinarian, was a completely mediocre choice for his post.

The day my father retired, Chief Secretary Mohan Mukherjee told him that the chief minister wanted him to continue and had already approved his re-appointment for two years. But with the prospect of many years of active life still ahead of him, Father had different plans. He told the chief secretary that he had already accepted a private sector offer and did not wish to continue in the government any longer. The chief secretary asked him to nevertheless see the chief minister before leaving office, but my father told him that he would rather avoid the embarrassment of having to turn down the request of the chief minister in person. He therefore paid him a visit a week later.

6

Building Post-Independence India

FATHER MISSED THE OPPORTUNITY to join politics and thus serve in a leadership role in the state. He was also denied the chance to become a member of the elite Indian Administrative Services, which robbed him of any prospects of reaching the top rank in his profession. Yet, he served the nation with distinction by first helping bring an end to the more-than-a-millennium-long hereditary rule in Mewar state and then contributing to the building of the state of Rajasthan immediately following its formation. He understood administration better than any of his colleagues, whether junior or senior, adhered to the highest standards of integrity, worked hard with clear focus, placed public interest above all else and had the courage of conviction. Unlike most of his colleagues, he read widely and kept abreast of all the important developments within the nation and internationally. A few highlights from his years in the state administration provide concrete evidence of his contributions to the well-being of the state and its people.

During the first term of Jai Narayan Vyas as Rajasthan chief minister, spanning 26 April 1951 to 3 March 1952, my father served as private secretary to Balwant Singh Mehta, minister of industries, mines and commerce. During this period, the issue of renewal of lease for mica mines to the influential industrialist Ramnath Podar came up. Twenty years earlier, the Maharaja of Jaipur had granted a twenty-year lease for the mines in the entire erstwhile state of Jaipur to the industrialist. The lease had a provision that it could be extended for another twenty years, subject to both parties agreeing. It had been a lucrative lease for the Podars; naturally, they wanted it extended. Accordingly, they applied for extension for another twenty years.

With a positive recommendation by the secretary, the Department of Mines and Geology recommended to the industries minister that the lease be renewed. When the thick file landed on the minister's desk, he asked my father to study it and prepare a summary of it for him. When my father carefully examined the file, he found that there had been a large number of complaints against the Podars for recovering mica through surface mining rather than deep mining. Moreover, after extracting mica, they had left the trenches and pits exposed and had not filled them back with sand. This had led to the creation of standing waterbodies during the rainy season, which served as breeding grounds for mosquitoes and resulted in the spread of malaria. My father was also aware that the new Constitution of the country disallowed private monopolies. He included these points in the summary he prepared for the minister, which led the latter to turn down the application from the Podars for renewal of their lease.

Mehta's decision created a bit of a stir in governmental as well as industry circles. The powerful industrialists' lobby denounced the government, arguing that after such treatment no industrialist would ever invest in the state. The Podars met the chief minister, who too was surprised by the industries minister's decision. He wrote to the minister stating that while he had no view on the merits of the case, it was incumbent upon him (the minister) to take the approval of the cabinet in a matter involving a lease of such large value. The minister replied saying that since the lease had been expiring, it had required no decision by the ministry. The ministry was simply taking possession of the mines on which the incumbent's lease had expired. Had the ministry wanted to renew the lease, a decision would have been required, and in that case he would have surely sought the approval of the cabinet. The chief minister had no choice but to accept the reply and did not pursue the matter further.

But the story did not end there. Ramnath Podar was a national-level industrialist with wide reach in the central government. He approached the Union minister for natural resources and scientific research, Sri Prakasa. The latter sent Minister Mehta a telegram, advising him to reconsider the matter to avoid a 'public scandal'. Mehta felt insulted and asked my father to draft a telegraphic reply to Sri Prakasa. Father drafted a sharply worded response, stating that the decision of the state government was in accordance with the provisions of the Constitution, and the matter being within the jurisdiction of the state, the Union government had no business interfering. The draft reply further stated that the state government strongly objected to the use of the expression 'public scandal' by the Union minister. When Father showed the draft reply to Mehta, the latter suggested clearing it with the chief minister. My father told him that the chief minister would never approve of such a reply, and a very different reply would have to go in that case. Mehta agreed, and approved dispatch of the draft at his own risk. My father had the telegram dispatched without the chief minister knowing about it. No follow-up reply came from the Union minister.

On the day the lease expired, the state government took over the mines with the beat of drums. It was then that my father sent the telegraphic correspondence between Sri Prakasa and Mehta to the secretary, Department of Mines and Geology. Soon, the correspondence became a subject of conversation among the officers and staff in the secretariat. When the chief minister heard of the matter, he congratulated Mehta for his courageous action. A few weeks later, Mehta went to Delhi to attend a conference where Sri Prakasa was present. To Mehta's surprise, the latter apologized to him, explaining that his officers had misled him on the matter. Sri Prakasa, a senior Congress leader at the national level, was known for his humility. When Mehta returned to Jaipur, he related the story to my father and thanked him for giving him the right advice at the right time.

By the time Sukhadia became chief minister of Rajasthan in November 1954, my father had already served as private secretary to three ministers. Though another minister in the Sukhadia regime wanted him to work with him, Father felt it was time for him to move on to one of the departments of the state government. Accordingly, he worked for the minister temporarily, until he could find a suitable replacement. That done, he asked the government for placement in one of the departments. As a stop-gap arrangement, he first served for three months in the appointments department and, beginning in March 1955, moved to a regular position as assistant secretary in the medical and health department. Hierarchy-wise, this was the third-ranked bureaucratic position within the department, with the position of deputy secretary immediately above and that of secretary at the top.

My father firmly believed that public money must be used with care and for the public good. He was also a courageous officer. Therefore, if he saw public money being misused, he would not hesitate to take necessary action, even if such action was against powerful individuals and carried the risk of personal harm. I recall asking him once whether it did not make for an uncomfortable existence for an officer if most of the others around him were corrupt while he tried to discharge his duties honestly. His reply was that it was always the other way around. The corrupt were the ones who feared the honest officers around them, even if they greatly outnumbered the latter.

Soon after my father joined the medical and health department, he had to deal with a difficult case of financial impropriety. It involved a highly influential medical doctor who also held a senior administrative position in the government. It was widely believed that the doctor knew Chief Minister Sukhadia well.

It so happened around this time that most district hospitals lacked X-ray equipment and also suffered from shortages of medicines. Therefore, the government had approved a sum of Rs 2.5 million for purchase of these items at the influential doctor's request. Though the doctor bought some medicines with the funds, he spent most of them on the purchase of a fleet of vehicles from a dealer who had been unable to sell it in the open market. Having spent the entire amount, the doctor submitted papers to the medical and health department for regularization of the purchase, ipso facto. The secretariat was a small place, and its corridors quickly became rife with speculation that there had been corruption in the transaction.

In the Indian bureaucratic system, a file begins its journey with the lowest-level official within the department and then moves up the hierarchy. Accordingly, the file containing the request for regularization of the expenditure eventually landed on my father's desk. When he examined it, he found that it was upon receiving an SOS from the doctor for the purchase of X-ray equipment and medicines for district hospitals that the revenue department had approved the sum of Rs 2.5 million. But the doctor had gone on to purchase vehicles to be used as ambulances in the district hospitals without any requisition from district medical health officers. Indeed, a number of district hospitals already had ambulances. Furthermore, he had purchased vehicles and medicines without so much as even seeking informal approval from any government official. My father recorded all these irregularities and stated in his tough note on the file that the purchases were wholly irregular and that the scarce resources provided by the revenue department had been wrongly utilized. He recommended that a high-powered committee needed to investigate the entire matter. He also recommended that the finance department be made aware of the case since the Office of the Accountant General would raise objections to the purchases in due course.

The file next went to the deputy secretary, whose first action was to show my father's note to the doctor. The latter was naturally very upset. The hapless deputy secretary held the file for some fifteen days and then submitted it to the secretary, with a note stating that the purchases were made in the public interest and therefore were worthy of regularization. The secretary called a meeting of the doctor, the deputy secretary and my father to sort out the matter. At the meeting, my father said that he had already recorded his views on the file and had nothing to add. The doctor defended himself, and the deputy secretary passionately supported him, arguing in favour of regularization of the purchases. The secretary patiently listened to all that the three had to say and later sent the file to the finance department, stating that the purchases were irregular and that the doctor needed to be pulled up.

In the finance department, the additional secretary examined the file and agreed with the view my father had put forth. He sent the file to the chief secretary, an ICS officer, recommending that an inquiry be set up to investigate the scandal. The chief secretary in turn called up my father and congratulated him for his courage in taking the side of truth without fear or favour. He sent the file to Chief Minister Sukhadia, advising that the inquiry be entrusted to a retired high court judge.

In the meantime, the doctor went to the chief minister and pressed him for my father's transfer. Having heard only one side of the story, the chief minister sent a note to the appointments department, asking them to move my father to another department. The chief secretary intervened, however, and told the chief minister that if officers were punished in this manner for doing what was right, they would be demoralized. Instead, they needed to be protected under such circumstances so that they could discharge their duties fearlessly. The chief minister got the message and dropped his instructions for the transfer.

His stand having been vindicated, my father went to the chief secretary a month later and requested that he be transferred to another department as a show of deference to the chief minister. The chief secretary saw merit in my father's suggestion and sent him first for training to the finance department in April 1957, and then moved him to the public works department in June 1957.

Later, as predicted by my father, the Accountant General included in his annual report a paragraph recommending action against the doctor for his transgression in spending Rs 2.5 million. But no action actually followed, perhaps because the doctor was to retire after a short while and had made invaluable contributions to the state in the line of his profession. He had been a pioneer in certain areas and hundreds of thousands of people in Rajasthan had benefited from his medical services.

Between June 1957 and October 1963, Father worked in three different departments: public works, irrigation and appointments. He made important contributions to the work of each department, but I will eschew their detailed discussion here. His next major venture worthy of detailed recall is the building of the Malviya Regional Engineering College, which is now known as Malviya National Institute of Technology and enjoys the status of an Institution of National Importance. The story of how my father got this institution off the ground in record time testifies to his ability to implement projects with great efficiency and at minimal cost to the taxpayer.

The second Five-Year Plan, covering the years 1956–57 to 1960–61, had envisaged numerous industrial projects. Implementation of these projects was critically dependent on the availability of qualified engineers. Keeping this in view, the central government had launched a scheme to establish a regional engineering college in each state. Accordingly, a decision was made to establish a regional engineering college in Jaipur. The government appointed Professor V.G. Garde, former principal of M.B.M. College in Jodhpur, as the principal of the new college, which was to be named Malviya Regional Engineering College. The chief secretary of Rajasthan, B.S. Mehta, asked my father if he would take on the challenge of getting the college built and started on time. His role would be that of officer on special duty (OSD) and first registrar of the institution. My father accepted the challenge and took over his new duties on 1 November 1963.

This is a period I distinctly remember. I was already eleven years old then and our home had served as an initial office of the proposed college. Even before Father had taken charge as OSD, letters from Garde had begun arriving at regular intervals at our home address. We children would diligently place these brown envelopes on Father's desk in his room for him to see when he came from the secretariat in the evening.

A small first batch of the proposed college in electrical and mechanical engineering had begun classes in the Birla Institute of Technology and Science in Pilani in July 1963. The plan was to start classes for this batch, and for a second batch to be admitted shortly, on 1 July 1964, in Jaipur. Therefore, my father had just eight months to put all the pieces of the puzzle in place. These pieces included an office, student admissions, faculty recruitment, hiring of office staff, as well as physical infrastructure including classrooms, hostels, laboratories and workshops, and equipment for the laboratories and workshops. Work had to be done simultaneously on all fronts and progress at breakneck speed to ensure that the deadline was met.

The first thing my father did was to find a suitable building available on rent to set up an office. He found one on Mahatma Gandhi Marg, which cuts Jawaharlal Nehru Marg perpendicularly at the Gandhi Circle, a short distance south of the main entrance to Rajasthan University. To make the office functional, he brought in two stenographers and two assistants on deputation from the secretariat and purchased two typewriters. He was now equipped to begin correspondence with the numerous entities with which he needed to deal over the next several months. The next important challenge was to find land on which temporary classrooms and hostel buildings could be built before he could look for a proper permanent site for the college.

It so happened that the government owned empty land opposite the office building he had rented. The state government planned to build houses for its employees on this land. My father asked Chief Secretary Mehta to spare that land for constructing temporary classrooms and hostels for the college, promising that the construction would be done in such a way that the buildings could be converted into employee housing once the college shifted to its permanent location. Mehta liked the idea and got the chief minister to agree. Construction began immediately, under the supervision of a brilliant engineer from the Public Works Department of the state government. Much to the amazement of everyone, construction was completed within four months. There remained the issue of the workshops, however. But it turned out that a well-equipped workshop at the nearby Podar Secondary

School had existed and remained unused for the past several years. All the college required was permission from the government to use it. The government, naturally, granted it.

Positions for faculty and administrative staff were advertised in parallel, and all recruitment was completed by the end of May 1964. All faculty members were in place by 15 June 1964. Furniture for the classrooms, offices and the hostels, and all equipment, including utensils, for the hostel kitchen, were purchased. Admissions for the second batch of the college were completed too. The batch that had studied in Pilani during 1963–64 moved to Jaipur. That batch and the new one began their classes as per schedule on 1 July 1964. In a country where the bureaucracy has been known to move at a snail's pace, my father successfully brought this first phase of the project to a conclusion at extraordinary speed. Both Principal Garde and Chief Secretary Mehta were mighty surprised and pleased.

With classes begun at the temporary site, my father turned to the second phase of the project. This involved creation of a permanent campus of the college. Principal Garde, himself a visionary, and my father felt that the permanent location of the college should be on a large enough piece of land so that its future expansion would not be constrained and it could have a shot at conversion into an Indian Institute of Technology. A committee chaired by Garde considered the matter in detail and concluded that the college ought to be located on a piece of land that was at least 150 acres in area. Luckily, my father found that a 200-acre piece of barren land existed on the southern boundary of Rajasthan University. Upon inspection, Garde, Mehta and the chief engineer of the Public Works Department agreed that this was the ideal tract of land on which to locate the permanent campus of the college.

The government had allotted the land to an individual a few years earlier, and it now needed to acquire it back from him. The authority for acquisition rested with the collector of Jaipur. My father knew him well. He met the latter and gave him the requisition letter. The collector acted fast. He invoked the emergency powers available under the then prevailing Land Acquisition Act and managed to complete all the formalities in a month's time. A compensation of Rs 56,000 to the owner was determined, which my father paid immediately on behalf of the college. Garde was deeply impressed by the speed of acquisition of the land and congratulated my father, who replied that the credit for it belonged to the collector, not him.

The next step for my father was to hire a firm to prepare a master plan for the college. A Delhi firm was selected and assigned the task. It completed the plan within six months, which the governing council of the college approved. Based on the plan, the central government allotted the necessary funds, and construction began on the main site of the college soon after. To shift the college to the permanent campus as soon as possible, priority was given to the main building, which had the classrooms and hostels. The office building was to be taken up the last. The plan was to shift the classes to the site on 1 July 1966.

Coincidentally, around this time Ravi decided to apply for admission to the college for the academic year 1965–66. He had been a meritorious student throughout, ranking eleventh and ninth in Rajasthan University in his pre-university and first-year BSc examinations, respectively. Therefore, he had no difficulty in getting admission to the college, which was strictly by merit.

The college had introduced two new branches of engineering – metallurgy and civil – in the year 1965–66. Ravi opted for the metallurgical branch for his degree.

In addition to overseeing construction of the new campus of the college, as registrar, my father was also in charge of its day-to-day administration. This occasionally brought him into conflict with one or two particularly contentious faculty members who would intrude into administrative matters. My father feared that these conflicts might lead the faculty members to become hostile towards him and that might eventually harm Ravi, which was the last thing he wanted. Additionally, he felt that with construction of the new campus well underway, he had been left with only the routine work of the registry. Therefore, rather than complete his three-year term as the OSD, he decided to return to the government early.

Accordingly, he informed Garde that he would soon be returning to the government. Garde was keen for him to stay two more years, but Father politely declined. Garde respected his decision, and my father left the college in October 1965. The government rewarded him with two months of privilege leave for the hard work he had put in to get the college on its feet. He was glad to have the break before resuming his duties at the secretariat. The concept of a vacation, in the sense of going to a resort or travelling to another part of the country, was non-existent in Jaipur in those days. Besides, even if such a concept had existed, a vacation would have been too costly for the family to afford. Since my father had a passion for books on contemporary politics and history and for the card game of bridge, those were the activities on which he chose to spend his relaxation time. At the end of his leave, in December 1965, he returned to the government, where he was appointed as assistant secretary in the revenue department.

The college successfully moved its classes to the main campus on 1 July 1966, as per plan. Beginning with his second year in the college, Ravi thus found himself on the main campus. It was a long commute for him to the college on bicycle, but he did it all diligently, completing his five years and earning the bachelor of engineering degree in 1970. As he had ranked fourth in his class, he got selected to serve on the faculty of the college as a lecturer. He served for four years before moving to the private sector, where he had an illustrious career.

I had left India for the United States on 1 September 1974 to pursue doctoral studies and therefore did not follow the progress of the college. But in December 2015, a full fifty years after my father had left it and Ravi had joined it, I had the privilege to visit it in my capacity as vice chairman of NITI Aayog, the think tank Prime Minister Narendra Modi had created as the successor institution to the erstwhile Planning Commission. It was deeply satisfying for me to see that the institution, with just four branches of engineering that my father had helped create, had evolved into a major technology institute. From Malviya Regional Engineering College, it had been rechristened Malviya National Institute of Technology (MNIT) in 2002. Five years later, in 2007, the central government recognized it as an Institution of National Importance, thereby conferring a considerable degree of autonomy of operation on it.

Today, MNIT boasts of thirteen engineering departments at eight centres of excellence for undergraduate studies, a school of management and twenty-seven specialized programmes for master's and doctoral studies. Its Centre for Advanced Design has nine well-equipped computer labs. The Vivekananda Lecture Theatre Complex has a combined capacity to accommodate 6,500 students. Its hostel now comfortably houses 5,000 students. In 2020, the National Institutional Ranking Framework ranked MNIT thirty-fifth among all engineering colleges in India.

When seen in today's context, it is difficult to believe that there was a time in independent India when a major academic institution could be built from scratch within eight months of appointment of the principal and registrar to the point of having full-fledged hostels and classrooms of its own. It is equally difficult to believe that in another two years the college could come to have its own brand-new campus on a two-hundred-acre piece of land that the government had to acquire from its owner. Today, our processes and procedures have become so multi-layered and complex that even the most efficient and empowered officers cannot accomplish in twice the time what my father accomplished in the mid 1960s. If my father had had to acquire the same land under the byzantine Land Acquisition Act of 2013, he would have had to extend his tenure as OSD by at least three years. Today, it is commonplace to see new colleges and universities struggle for several years, not only for acquisition of land but also for building their campus.

In the revenue department, my father was given charge of two sections: jagirs and forests. There was very little work related to jagirs at the level of the secretariat. But the case with forests turned out to be quite different. Here, he found himself defending the public interest in yet another important case. As a consequence, he infuriated the forest minister, who saw to it that he was immediately transferred to another department.

Fundamentally, the case had its origins in the fact that India lacks conclusive land titles. All it has are revenue records and records of purchase and sales of land between buyer and seller, carried out on stamp papers issued by the government. Also called settlement records, revenue records go back to the British government days when the latter began keeping such records on a systematic basis for fixing responsibility for land tax. The records are not always up to date, however. For instance, the person recorded as the owner of a piece of land in the settlement records may sell it to someone else. Even if they register the sale with the registration office, the revenue records may not get updated. For reasons such as these, courts do not accept revenue records as the final proof of ownership, and as a result property disputes throughout India are common. In 2016, Rajasthan became the first state to enact a law known as the Rajasthan Urban Land (Certification of Titles) Act, under which conclusive land titles may be issued. But few owners have been issued such titles to date.

The case that landed on my father's desk involved a two-hundred-acre piece of forest land located east and south of Malviya Regional Engineering College, which was still under construction. A private individual had claimed ownership of this land on the basis of an entry in the old settlement records. He submitted an application with a certified copy of the relevant entry in the settlement records to the minister in charge of forests, Bhikhabhai Bhil, requesting transfer of the land. In the application, he alleged that the forest department of the former Jaipur state had occupied the land in an unauthorized manner. Rather than obtain a report from the chief conservator of forests (CCF) or the forest department in the secretariat, the minister passed an order for the handing over of the land in question to the applicant within three days.

The file containing the order came for compliance from the minister to the secretary of the revenue department, who in turn sent it to my father. When my father saw the order, he was in a state of shock. The land had not been of much value in the pre-Independence era under Jaipur state. But having just helped build the engineering college adjacent to this land, he knew that this land now had huge public value. He immediately requested the CCF to dig out the relevant file from the records of the former state of Jaipur and send it to him. The CCF complied with the request the very next morning. When my father examined the file, he found that the land in question had been entered in the name of the forefathers of the applicant in the settlement record of 1890. In subsequent years, the settlement records reported it as Crown land. It was likely that, having no use for the barren land, the applicant's forefathers had abandoned it. The applicant had no papers to show that he or his forefathers had ever paid rent for it. He had filed a claim for ownership of the land to the forest officer when the former Jaipur state began proceedings to bring the land under an afforestation scheme. But Jaipur state had rejected that claim. The applicant had then approached the collector, Jaipur, of the former Jaipur state government, and finally the high court, but was rebuffed by all.

After the formation of the state of Rajasthan, the applicant had filed a fresh application before the settlement officer, Jaipur, seeking entry of his name against the land in question on the basis of the 1890 entry in the former Jaipur state settlement records. The section officer followed the routine practice of issuing a show-cause notice to the state government for why the applicant's claim should be denied. Evidently, no one in the state government had

My father at the Rajasthan Secretariat in 1959, seated on the right of Chief Minister Mohan Lal Sukhadia (*centre*).

My father (*extreme right*, in a half-sweater) welcoming PM Jawaharlal Nehru to Suwana, 9 March 1959.

With Prime Minister Indira Gandhi at the launch of his book *Rajasthan Ka Itihas*, 2 March 1983. *L–R*: Ashok Panagariya (my brother), historian and UGC Chairman Dr Satish Chandra, my father, Rajasthan Finance Minister Chandan Mal Baid and Rajasthan Education Minister Surendra Vyas.

With Vice President of India Bhairon Singh Shekhawat (*left*) and Chief Minister of Rajasthan Shiv Charan Mathur (*centre*), January 1981.

Gifting copies of his books to Chief Minister Ashok Gehlot.

Chief Minister Hari Dev Joshi honouring my father with the award for the best book on the freedom struggle in Rajasthan by the Rajasthan Hindi Granth Academy, 1985, for *Rajasthan mein Swantantrata Sangram.*

The Panagariya house in Suwana, Rajasthan, with a grand platform, January 1981. The dome of Charbhuja Temple can be seen on the left.

The Baloo Lal Panagariya public library in Suwana, built in memory of my father.

My parents with their entire family at the celebration of their fiftieth wedding anniversary, 1984. Front row (*L–R*): Grandchildren Meghna, Nidhi, Arushi and Aditi. Middle row: Father and Mother in the centre flanked by daughter Prem Lata (with my son Ananth Hirsh in her lap) and her husband. Back row (*L–R*): I, my sister-in-law Asha and my brother Ravi, my brother Ashok and his wife Meena, my wife Amita, sister Kamala, and Prem Lata's children Avinash and Anjula.

Surrounded by his grandchildren, 1994. (*L–R*): Ajay, Arihant (in Father's lap), Ananth Hirsh, with Arushi and Aditi at the back.

paid any attention to the notice. The section officer had then issued an order for entry of the name of the applicant against the land in the settlement records. It was on the basis of this entry that the applicant had approached the minister to seek possession of the land.

My father wrote a long note narrating the full history of the case. He pointed out that the former Jaipur state government and the highest judicial court of the state had rejected the applicant's claim and that an entry in the settlement records could not serve as conclusive evidence of ownership. He further stated that the land now being worth more than Rs 10 million, a final decision should be taken only after consultation with the law department and finance department.

After examining the note written by my father, the secretary of the revenue department was left with no option but to send the file to the law department. The latter concurred with my father's view. When Minister Bhikhabhai Bhil learned of what had transpired in the matter, he was furious. He called my father to his office and told him to be prepared to face the consequences of going against his decision. My father politely replied that in order to protect himself as a public servant, he had no choice in the matter.

The fallout from the incident for my father was that the government immediately transferred him out of the revenue department to the operations and management (O&M) department. Rather than wait for the appointment of his successor in the revenue department, Father handed over the charge immediately to the section officer and assumed his duties in the newly assigned department. It was unfortunate that the secretary and the chief secretary turned out to be too timid to come to the defence of a junior officer who acted fearlessly to protect the public interest.

Though my father was punished for defying his minister, valuable public land was saved from being grabbed by a private individual. In due course, Malviya Nagar, a beautiful residential colony, sprang up on this land. Today, even a 250 square metre plot in the colony goes for Rs 20 million. One can guess the enormous value of the two hundred acres that Father was able to save from unlawful possession by a private individual.

This episode brings into sharp relief the cost India and Indians pay on a continuous basis for lacking a system of conclusive legal ownership titles to immovable property. The owner of any such property in India has undisputed ownership right to it only so long as no one disputes it. A challenge to ownership rights can be mounted by almost anyone at any time, with a prolonged court battle almost guaranteed. The result has been the accumulation of millions of land disputes around the country over time, with concomitant costs in terms of economic efficiency and growth.

Any large-scale enterprise requires a large piece of land. Given the large number of ownership disputes in existence in India, assembling such a piece of land is a real challenge for an entrepreneur, even when she is willing to pay the market price for such land. With multiple claimants to at least a number of parcels of land within any contiguous piece of fifty to hundred acres, the buyer does not know whom to buy those parcels from. In most countries with weak or no land title systems, the government can solve the problem by acquiring such parcels of land on behalf of the entrepreneur. But in 2013, India adopted a highly restrictive Land Acquisition Act, which makes it extremely difficult for the government to acquire land on behalf of a private enterprise. Therefore, in addition to inflexible labour laws, land markets too have become a major constraint to the growth of large-scale enterprises in India.

The O&M department was directly under Chief Secretary Mehta, whom my father had known for a long time. Within a few months of Father joining this department, Mehta retired. He had served in this position for eight years, from May 1958 to October 1966, with a break of one year in between. He was extremely popular among the secretariat staff, and they gave him a rousing farewell, with the chief minister and most of the members of his cabinet attending the event.

My brothers and I have always believed that Mehta was the villain in the matter of our father's career in the Government of Rajasthan. Father had served in the state of Rajasthan since its inception, and in the United State of Rajasthan prior to that. He had been known for his impeccable administrative skills, efficiency, integrity and courage throughout the secretariat. Mehta too had observed his functioning first-hand, since the appointments department, where my father had served from July 1960 to October 1963, was directly under him. Yet, after more than sixteen years of service at the time of Mehta's retirement, my father had not been given a single promotion. Indeed, according to Ravi, who once overheard Father talking confidentially with a friend, his name had come up for promotion once during Mehta's tenure as chief secretary. But Mehta turned it down, noting on the file that he was too junior to be promoted.

Yet, never once did my siblings or I hear Father utter a single critical word about Mehta. His unfair treatment at Mehta's hands notwithstanding, Father remained full of admiration for him. He always spoke of him with utmost respect and applauded his many attributes and accomplishments. He would always credit him for the lead Rajasthan had taken in establishing Panchayati Raj in all of India. He would note with admiration how Mehta gave priority to elected representatives such as panchas, pradhans and zila pramukhs over bureaucrats. He also took pride in pointing out that he was the first bureaucrat in the country to be honoured by the President of India with the Padma Shri.

In contrast to Mehta, his successor, Chief Secretary K.P.U. Menon, took no time to formally recognize my father's talents and contributions. He joined on 29 October 1966, and by January 1967 had promoted my father to the position of deputy secretary. Fortunately, immediately upon taking charge as chief secretary, Menon had appointed my father as staff welfare officer in addition to his charge as assistant secretary, O&M. In this new role, my father quickly attended to the grievances of numerous employees and pensioners. He resolved the cases of dozens of retirees that had remained pending for years. In a similar vein, he expedited the cases of seniority, pay fixation and promotion of a number of employees. That was sufficient for Menon to recognize his value as an officer and reward him with the promotion. The secretariat staff celebrated my father's promotion with great joy. We, the family members, got a hint of it when a member of his staff brought home a large stock of garlands in the evening. It was a great moment of joy and pride for us all.

My father's first appointment as deputy secretary was in the Department of Education. This meant that he had to move out of the chief secretary's office. Menon had been so pleased with his work as staff welfare officer, however, that he asked him to continue to serve in that role. But that arrangement did not work very well. Therefore, rather than relieve him of his duties as staff welfare officer, Menon brought him back to his office as deputy secretary, Cabinet. Father worked in the twin roles for the following three years.

In January 1970, the government appointed my father as secretary of the newly formed State Agro Industries Corporation. Chandan Mal Baid, a former minister in the Sukhadia cabinet and a future finance minister of the state, served as the chairman of the corporation. A key function of the corporation was the allocation of tractors among potential buyers. Imports of all products in India were subject to strict licencing in those days. As far as the sale of imported tractors in Rajasthan was concerned, only the corporation had the licence to import a fixed number of them each year. Therefore, it enjoyed a monopoly over their sales. But, being a public-sector entity, the corporation had to sell the tractors on a no-profit-no-loss basis. That in turn meant that the number of those wishing to buy tractors far exceeded the number of tractors available. Therefore, some rule had to be devised to select buyers from amongst the applicants.

This situation carried great potential for corruption as well as prospects for charges of corruption, even if no corruption actually took place. Luckily, both Chairman Baid and my father were individuals of great integrity. Together, they decided that the most transparent way to allocate the tractors would be by public lottery. Accordingly, they opted to allot 95 per cent of the tractors by lottery. They left allotment of the remaining 5 per cent of tractors to the discretion of the chairman. This was done in anticipation of demands from influential politicians, as is common in India whenever non-price mechanisms are applied to allocate something in short supply.

The full transparency of the system notwithstanding, members of the Legislative Assembly (MLAs) in the Opposition took no time in alleging that there was corruption in the allotment of tractors and that tractors were being diverted to Pakistan. The speaker of the Legislative Assembly at the time was N.N. Acharya, who had served alongside my father in the United State of Rajasthan government and had chosen to return to politics after the formation of the state of Rajasthan. Responding to the uproar, he appointed a committee of fifteen MLAs to investigate the matter. The leader of the Opposition, Bhairon Singh Shekhawat, who later served multiple terms as the chief minister of Rajasthan and one term as vice president of India, acted as the chairman of the committee.

The committee examined my father's role in the allocation for three days straight, looking into the allotment of each and every tractor, whether by lottery or through the discretionary quota of the chairman. It could not find a single case of allotment by lottery that was not according to the set rules and procedures. As for allotment under the discretionary quote, every single tractor was found to be allotted to worthy individuals who had agricultural land, with no sign of any corruption. My father also pointed out to the committee that some of its members themselves had received tractors through the chairman's discretionary quota.

With no adverse findings, the matter ended there, and the committee was dissolved. It was so embarrassed that it did not even submit a report. Later, when my father asked one of the

MLAs on the committee why they had failed to submit a report, he sheepishly answered that the report in this case would have only benefited the ruling party. After that episode, no questions were raised on any matter related to the corporation during the time Baid and my father were still presiding over it.

Elections to the Legislative Assembly were held in July 1972. By this time, in July 1971, Indira Gandhi had already ousted Sukhadia as chief minister and sent him as governor to the state of Karnataka (then called Mysore) for having sided with her opponents in the 1969 presidential elections. Barkatullah Khan, another Congress leader, now served as the chief minister. In the elections, the Congress scored a big victory, winning two-thirds of all seats in the Assembly. Baid also won his election and was appointed the finance minister of the state.

During his tenure at the Agro Industries Corporation, Baid had developed unshakeable confidence in the ability and integrity of my father as an officer. Therefore, unsurprisingly, upon becoming the finance minister, he picked Father to be the deputy secretary in the finance department. From June 1972 till his retirement on 30 June 1976, Father worked in this department. He found these four years to be the most exciting of the more than twenty-five years he spent in the government. In addition to the sensitive excise department, he held the charge of state insurance, local fund audit and accounts services during these years.

Among the challenges in the excise department, the biggest one was of raising adequate volumes of revenue. The main source of excise revenue in the state was the tax on country liquor. In the many years prior to my father's taking charge of the department, the big liquor contractors had systematically pushed out the small contractors, thereby stamping out a key source of competition. With the big contractors relatively few in number, they were able to form a cartel of sorts. They would grease the palms of the officials and contribute generously to the election campaigns of politicians to maintain their stranglehold on the sector. While their profits soared, excise revenues suffered. They came to have a determining influence on not just the state excise policy but also on the postings and transfers of excise officials who implemented the policy.

At the instance of the big contractors, the state had adopted a policy of auctioning of liquor shops in groups instead of individually. By definition, small contractors lacked the resources to bid for a bundle of multiple shops. Big traders then colluded to distribute the different clusters of shops among themselves at bid prices that they had already negotiated between themselves. The auction was thus only in name. Despite the manifold increase in the consumption of liquor in the state, excise revenues had remained static. Baid, the new finance minister, felt that this was an unacceptable situation.

The finance department took the decision to break the cartel of the liquor barons. My father dropped the policy of auctioning shops in lots and began auctioning the shops individually. That immediately drew a large number of players into the auctions. The excise revenue went up from the Rs 80–90 million of earlier years to Rs 120 million in 1972–73. Finance Minister Baid was pleased by this success, but not for long.

It was inevitable that the big traders would mount a counter-attack. Their opportunity came when the government opened auctions for the following year, 1973–74. On the eve of the auction, the traders announced that they would boycott it. The result was that only the small shops got taken, with no bids coming for the liquor shops in large cities such as Jaipur, Ajmer, Kota and Ganganagar. The stakes were high for the government, since the shops in these large cities contributed the lion's share of the excise revenue.

With the finance minister firmly behind him, my father was not about to back down. He decided to let the state-owned Ganganagar Sugar Mills run the shops for which no bids had come. Of course, the running of liquor shops hardly being the business of a state-owned public sector enterprise, the government experienced a sizeable loss of revenue. The policy came under criticism, but my father refused to yield. Soon the contractors' lobby began sending feelers for reconciliation, but he paid no heed to them.

In February 1974, the government began preparing for the auction of shops for year 1974–75. Anticipating that the big contractors might boycott it once again, this time around Father decided to invite some of the big contractors from Uttar Pradesh and Haryana to bid for them. That proved to be the undoing of the contractors' lobby. All the big contractors returned to the table. The ensuing intense competition brought the state a whopping Rs 190 million in excise revenues. The increase more than made up for the tiny loss incurred the previous year. The following year, 1975–76, revenue went up further, to Rs 210 million, without any increase in the quantity of liquor issued from the state warehouse to the contractors. The liquor barons did not raise their heads again, at least till my father retired from the government.

As deputy secretary in charge of state insurance, my father faced a different challenge. A director, assisted by half a dozen junior officers, headed the operations of this department. All of them, including the director, had risen from the ranks, and from within the department. Therefore, they had difficulty exercising control over their former colleagues, who were represented by a powerful employees' union. In late 1973, the union went on a lightning strike, meaning, they struck work without any prior notice. Their principal demand was for the removal of the director. With Barkatullah Khan having died unexpectedly due to a heart attack in October 1973, the veteran politician Hari Dev Joshi was the chief minister at this time. He intervened directly and accepted the employees' demand. The director of State Insurance was removed. But that raised the question of his succession. No IAS or even RAS officer was willing to take the hot seat. In the end, the finance minister asked my father to take charge of the department in addition to his other duties.

My father remained the director of state insurance for one year while looking after other departments in his portfolio. During this year, he solved nearly all the problems of the staff, filled a large number of vacancies at the clerical level, put officers on their toes and restored discipline among the employees. He did this without recourse to harsh measures such as suspension, demotion and dismissal.

The key to bringing order to the department turned out to be the transfer of a few dozen 'black sheep' employees to places where the department had limited operations. That narrowed the scope of damage that these employees could do to the department's work by vitiating the work environment. As is common in the Indian system, Father came under pressure to cancel some of the transfers. He knew that if he reversed even a single decision, the powerful employees' union would see to it that he reversed all his decisions.

Unfortunately, however, among the 'black sheep' he transferred was the son of the chief minister's brother. When the brother knocked on the chief minister's door to have the transfer cancelled, the latter called my father to his office and asked him to do the needful. My father explained to the chief minster that if he were to cancel his nephew's transfer, the employees' union would be up in arms and force him to cancel all transfers. The progress he was making in bringing discipline to the department would then be wiped out in one stroke.

To his credit, the chief minister understood the problem and concurred with my father. He immediately turned to his brother and told him to advise his son to work hard in his new position, else he might face the prospect of being transferred yet again to a truly distant and isolated place such as Jaisalmer or Barmer. The matter ended there. To my father's good fortune, this story leaked out and had a salutary effect on the union and employees. They understood that my father meant business. Every employee, without exception, joined his new position by the stipulated date. The authority of the director was re-established and employees returned to performing their assigned duties. That in turn brought relief to hundreds of retired employees who had been waiting to be paid the insurance amounts due to them.

Another reform worth a brief mention, which my father was able to implement to the benefit of the state employees and pensioners, concerned the role of the accountant general in the disbursal of salaries and pensions. Whenever an officer was transferred, went on leave, earned annual increment or was promoted, the accountant general was required to issue a new pay-slip. Similarly, the accountant general had to sanction the pensions of all retirees, from Class IV employees all the way up to the chief secretary. Unfortunately, the office of the accountant general was notorious for delays in discharging these routine duties. It took numerous trips by the employee and the pensioner to the office to get new payslips issued or pensions sanctioned. This was particularly burdensome in the case of employees living in cities other than Jaipur, where the office of the accountant general was located.

Upon reviewing the Accounts Code, my father discovered that it was up to the state government to give the authority to issue payslips and sanction pensions to the accountant general and that it had the power to withdraw such authority. But setting aside one or two states, none had shown the courage to exercise that authority. My father advised the government to withdraw the authority from the accountant general. Initially there was some hesitation, but the government eventually concurred with my father's proposal. Once it made the decision, it immediately withdrew its authority to the accountant general to issue payslips. It took a little longer in the case of the accountant general's authority to sanction pensions, since the number of cases involved was rather large. But both reforms got implemented, bringing relief to a vast number of employees and pensioners.

As deputy secretary in charge of accounts services, Father also worked to bring justice to the Rajasthan Accounts Services officers. He discovered that no effort had been made to establish seniority among these officers for a very long time. The result had been that no Departmental Promotion Committee (DPC) had met to consider promotions for these employees since as far back as 1956. Father got the seniority established in consultation with the Public Service Commission and got the DPC appointed to decide on promotions of officers. The DPC finally confirmed a large number of officers who had been officiating in senior positions for many years.

The story of my father's contribution to the betterment of the lives of people will be incomplete without a discussion of the role he played in the development of his village, Suwana. This was the place where he was born, where he spent the precious years of his childhood and saw his mother struggle with dignity and pride. The village and its people always remained very dear to him. He would often tell my mother that the land of Suwana was very dear to him and that he intended to return to settle there after retirement. That, of course, did not happen, but he did the next best thing: use every opportunity that came his way to develop the village and improve the lives of the villagers.

It may be recalled that as early as 1943, at the initiative of the Mewar Praja Mandal, he had helped establish the rural-oriented Gram Vidyalaya (village school). In addition to providing education to children in Suwana and nearby villages, that school became a focal point of many social and cultural activities. The school hosted such eminent scholars as Ramnath Suman and Makhanlal Chaturvedi. Mewar Praja Mandal leader Manikya Lal Verma visited the school many times. Even the great Sarvodaya leader Jayaprakash Narayan came to speak at a Sarvodaya conference that the village hosted. His ninety-minute speech at the event left a deep impression on my father.

After the formation of the full state of Rajasthan, Father had joined its first government as private secretary to Bhure Lal Baya, the minister for the Public Works Department (PWD). The government had decided that it should build one pucca road in every region of the state. My father suggested to Baya that in Mewar region, priority be given to linking the granary in Uparmal, where Bijolia was located, to Bhilwara. This would provide better connect to foodgrain producers and consumers. The proposal was in the overall public interest, but for my father it also offered the side benefit of bringing the first pucca road to his village, since it lay on the route between Uparmal and Bhilwara.

In 1955, as assistant secretary in the Medical and Health Department, Father was able to get an Ayurvedic dispensary sanctioned for the village. He then began working on getting a post office and a public call office (PCO) opened in the village. This required prolonged correspondence with the central government, but he was eventually successful in getting both done for the village.

In February 1959, Prime Minister Jawaharlal Nehru had planned a visit to Bhilwara. Father thought that this was a good opportunity to bring him to the village. He met Manikya Lal Verma and lobbied him to include a visit to Suwana in Nehru's itinerary. Being fond of Suwana, Verma agreed, on the condition that my father would take full responsibility for making the arrangements. Verma got Nehru to agree.

Father went to Suwana and took charge of all arrangements for Nehru's visit. The visit took place on the morning of 9 March. Nehru came at 8 a.m. sharp, with Verma and Chief Minister Sukhadia accompanying him. The villagers welcomed him with a one-sentence welcome address inscribed in golden letters on a silken cloth:

'Bharat ke Hriday Samrat Pt. Jawaharlal Nehru ka Suwana ki Janata Hardik Abhinandan Karti hai.'

['The People of Suwana Welcome the King of Indian Hearts, Pandit Jawaharlal Nehru'].

The warmth of the villagers visibly pleased Nehru. He addressed the large gathering for fifteen minutes, had breakfast with the several hundred villagers and left at 9 a.m.

Verma and Sukhadia were pleased with the successful visit and thanked my father. Sukhadia then asked if the state could do anything for the village. Not one to ever miss an opportunity to advance the cause of his village, Father asked the chief minister to bring electricity to the village. Sukhadia agreed, and within three months, Suwana had electricity. It became the first village to be electrified in Rajasthan after the formation of the state. The impact on the people was deep. The Congress won their hearts forever. The village remains loyal to the party to this day. Even during the 1977 elections following the Emergency, it voted for the Congress.

On 2 October 1959, Rajasthan introduced Panchayati Raj. My father met Verma and pleaded with him that Suwana should be considered as the location for the Panchayat Samiti of Bhilwara. It was an ideal choice, he felt. Verma once again obliged Father and asked Sukhadia to consider the matter. Alongside, Father also spoke to Chief Secretary Mehta, who was in charge of Panchayati Raj institutions and with whom he had a good working relationship. The state government eventually granted my father's request, and Suwana is now the headquarters of the Bhilwara Panchayat Samiti.

The next facility for the village was the supply of piped water. Father successfully got Suwana included among the villages where piped water supply would be installed in the 1973 annual plan. Accordingly, Suwana got piped water supply in 1974. The same year, with the help of Dada Bhai, who happened to be the MLA from Bhilwara, Father could get Suwana an allopathic dispensary and a veterinary outpost.

My father now felt that the village needed a high school. Once again, he made a push for it at the relevant places and got a high school established. All the children from Gram Vidyalaya shifted to the Government High School, and the Vidyalaya was closed. The Government High School later became a higher secondary, and finally a senior higher secondary school.

Before my father retired from the state government on 30 June 1976, he saw to it that Suwana had all the basic amenities that the government could provide.

Retirement from the government, of course, did not mean retirement from professional life. An eternal optimist, Father decided to launch a whole new career as an author in the years that followed. Given the life expectancy at the time, he must have scarcely realized that this career would turn out to be just as long as the one he had in the government of Rajasthan.

During his stints with *Lokvani* and *Mewar Praja Mandal Patrika*, Father had discovered his talent and passion for writing. Therefore, at the personal level, he found this second career yet more fulfilling than his first. I used to return home for extended visits during the summers almost every other year for nearly two decades after his retirement. On those visits, he and I would sit on the lawn in the front yard of the house under the shade of tall trees and discuss for hours his writing projects of the previous two years and those on the horizon. His passion and excitement for what he was doing never diminished. Memories of those precious moments spent with him shall forever remain etched in my memory.

7

New Horizons: An Author and a Historian

ASSISTED BY THE THRIFTINESS of my mother that matched his own, Father had been able to plan his finances well. Until he retired, the family was dependent exclusively on his salary, which was not very much in those days. High salaries, which today attract even qualified engineers and PhD holders towards Class IV government jobs, came many years after his retirement. I would dare speculate that his pension at the time of his passing away in 2006 exceeded, in real terms, the last salary he drew in active service by a significant margin. It is testimony to the sound management of finances by him and Mother that at the time of retirement he had no liabilities whatsoever left to discharge. Instead, they had enough assets to carry them for the remainder of their lives, with all their children able to support themselves.

Father deposited the gratuity, provident fund and insurance money received upon retirement in a bank account. The pension and interest income from these funds were more than enough for his and Mother's simple living. Indeed, they could have chosen to treat themselves to a few luxuries since Father now had another source of income from a job with a business house that he had accepted a week before he retired. But the only luxury he allowed himself was a post-retirement job that would use up no more than a day's time per week, leaving him free to pursue other interests.

Back in 1946, Karpoor Chandra Kulish, editor of *Rajasthan Patrika*, had worked with my father as a proofreader at *Lokvani*. Later, in 1956, he had launched the *Patrika,* which in due course displaced its competitor *Rashtradoot* as the top daily in the state. Though *Dainik Bhaskar*, launched in Rajasthan in the mid 1990s, challenged its supremacy, *Patrika* remained popular, not just in Rajasthan but also in much of the Hindi heartland of India. In July 2017, it had the formidable circulation of 3.5 million and it had editions in multiple cities in seven states as well as in Delhi. Upon learning that my father had just retired, Kulish approached him and extended him an invitation to write for *Patrika.* For my father, the invitation could not have come at a more opportune time.

During his last four years with the government, Father had worked in the Department of Finance and had acquired intimate knowledge of the state's economy and finances. He was disappointed, however, that hardly anyone wrote on this subject in the media. Therefore, his first thought was to contribute articles on economy and finance. But upon reflection, he came to the conclusion that the readership for these subjects would be small, even in a city like Jaipur, and it would be difficult to keep it engaged beyond eight to ten articles per year. He wanted a subject that would have wider appeal and could keep readers engaged on a regular basis for at least a few years. Keeping these considerations and his own expertise in view, he eventually settled on the history of Rajasthan as the subject of his articles. Having observed and experienced it first-hand, he felt that he was uniquely positioned to provide a perspective on princely rule in Mewar, the formation of the United State of Rajasthan, and then greater Rajasthan.

In the following two years, Father wrote more than a hundred articles on the history of Rajasthan. He became a 'hit' with the readers, who flooded the 'Letters to the Editor' section in the *Patrika* with comments on his articles. Occasionally, he also wrote articles on the state's economy and finances. Contrary to his original expectation, these too proved popular. In particular, they got the attention of the political class. Soon, the finance minister and the leader of the Opposition began visiting him around the time of the state budget. On one occasion, they both wanted to come the same day. To avoid the embarrassment of having them run into each other at his home, Father had to schedule one meeting in the morning and the other in the evening!

For a serious writer, writing is a means to learning. I began writing on Indian economic policy on a regular basis in the media in 1999. Because of my scholarly work in the field, I had a deep understanding of economics. Even so, I rarely write an op-ed without thorough research of the facts and what other informed authors have written earlier on the subject of my piece. The process results in much learning and greater clarity of thought on the subject. The stock of knowledge so created feeds into future scholarly writings that take the form of longer articles and books.

I suspect that as my father wrote articles in the *Patrika* on the history of Rajasthan, he underwent a similar process of learning.

To verify facts, he had to read books on the subject and consult other reliable sources. As this process progressed, his stock of knowledge grew. By 1980, he had reached a stage where he felt confident that he could now try his hands at a book on the history of Rajasthan. He derived courage and inspiration from the fact that many distinguished historians of Rajasthan, including Muhnot Nainsi, James Tod, Kaviraj Shyamaldas and Gaurishankar Hirachand Ojha, had come from the ranks of administrators. He felt that the existing books were often bulky, revolved around the ruling houses, neglected the socioeconomic and cultural aspects of people's lives and lacked the contemporary context. Therefore, he felt he could make a real contribution by providing a compact history of Rajasthan that was more inclusive and extended to recent events leading to the transition from princely rule to the modern-day state of Rajasthan.

That ambition eventually translated into not one but four books on the history of Rajasthan, two in Hindi and two in English. The first of these books was *Rajasthan ka Itihas* (A History of Rajasthan), which was a compact 350-page account of the state's history from ancient times till 1956. It was published in 1982. The book was formally released by Prime Minister Indira Gandhi on 2 March 1983. The release function at the Prime Minister's Office, then located at 1, Akbar Road in New Delhi, was a low-key affair, but the mere fact of Gandhi's involvement in it was enough to attract the attention of the media on a wide scale. The following summer, Amita and I came to Jaipur to offer our newborn son Hirsh's hair, still uncut, to Balaji of Sindri. When Father and I got to sit together on the lawn in the front yard of the house to chat, he told me the story of the visit to the Prime Minister's Office and the release of his book with great excitement. Referring to the publicity that book got in the press the following day, he said, 'Thanks to it, I became a "historian" overnight.'

At a personal level, the release event was a source of immense pride and pleasure for my father. Indira Gandhi was the leader he had admired the most. Even her imposition of Emergency in 1975 had not diminished his admiration for her. He had dedicated his very first book to her in these glowing terms, 'Respectfully dedicated to India's Prime Minister Mrs Indira Gandhi who added a golden chapter to the nation's history by inflicting bitter defeat on the enemy on his own soil in the Bangladesh War.'

Distinguished historian Satish Chandra, the finance and education ministers of Rajasthan and my brother Ashok were present at the release function. I regretted that being in the United States at the time, I missed the opportunity. But I got my consolation prize in the form of a copy of the book, from which I did the above translation of the dedication. Affixed on the top right-hand corner of the dedication page of this copy is the familiar autograph of Prime Minister Indira Gandhi in Hindi, with the release date noted right below it in her handwriting. By a strange coincidence, the copy of the book I picked from my father's collection after he passed away turned out to be the one Mrs Gandhi had autographed for him.

When Mrs Gandhi released my father's first book, she had asked him whether he had covered the history of the freedom movement in Rajasthan. Though he was able to answer her question in the affirmative, he felt that the solitary chapter in the book on the subject had not done justice to it. The topic required a full-scale book-length treatment. Upon inquiring, he found out that following Independence, the state government had tried to get an authentic book written on the subject. It had even commissioned, successively, three leading historians from the state to do it, placing substantial financial resources at their disposal. But none had been able to deliver. Father decided to undertake the task on his own without approaching the state government.

The project proved a real challenge since there was no major work on the subject on which he could draw. The states department had created Rajasthan by merging as many as twenty-two independent states in 1948–49. It was a Herculean task to collect material on all of them. To Father's good fortune, however, he got two bags full of old newspapers published from Ajmer and Jodhpur from Jodhpur Praja Mandal leader Chaganraj Chopasani Wala. Those newspapers proved a goldmine of information. Having also had direct association with the freedom movement, he knew a number of freedom fighters personally. He collected a good bit of information from them too. He also went to personally meet several others whom he could identify as having been a part of the freedom movement. But he found that barring two or three out of this group, everyone wanted to talk at length about himself without providing concrete documentation of his contribution.

It took Father a good two and a half years to piece together all the material into a coherent narrative. He titled the resulting book *Rajasthan mein Swatantrata Sangram* (The Freedom Movement in Rajasthan). National Publishing House in New Delhi, which had published *Rajasthan ka Itihas*, was going to publish the book, but before it could proceed Rajasthan Chief Minister Hari Dev Joshi came to know of the manuscript. He immediately called Father and told him to withdraw it from the publisher. He wanted the State Hindi Granth Academy to publish it. With some difficulty, Father was able to rescue the manuscript from his publisher and give it to the academy.

The academy published the book, and Joshi gifted the first copy of it to Rajiv Gandhi, then prime minister of India, on 2 October 1985. Gandhi had come to Jaipur that day to inaugurate the centenary celebrations of the founding of the Indian National Congress. For my father, this was the next best thing to gifting the first copy to Indira Gandhi, who had been the inspiration behind the book but had fallen to her assassins' bullets a year earlier.

Predictably, the book was a huge success. Being the only book on the important subject, and carefully written after serious research on primary sources of information, it quickly became the bible in its field. Long back, the state government had announced a cash prize for the best book on the freedom struggle in the state. The book easily won that prize, with the state government honouring Father at a function attended by the chief minister and other distinguished leaders. The second edition of the book came out in 1988, and the third in 1998. The academy also published a paperback version of the book in 1998. The book continues to generate a small amount in royalty every year. I received the latest instalment of my share in it while writing this biography.

Father's next book was in English, titled *State Politics in India,* and was published in 1988. It was an account of political developments in the state of Rajasthan, beginning with its formation in 1948–49. It also dealt with Centre-state relations and offered a discussion of electoral reforms. Once again, this was among the early book-length accounts of political developments in Rajasthan since Independence and, at the time, the only up-to-date history of Rajasthan state politics. Unsurprisingly, it quickly acquired a wide readership. Many master's programmes in political science still recommend the book for their courses. Along with

Rajasthan Ka Itihas, it is widely used by aspirants of various state services, including the Rajasthan Administrative Services.

During the 1990s, Father wrote four other books: on the socio-cultural and economic history of Rajasthan; on the polity and economy in Rajasthan; on the history of Kashmir; and on the Indian economy. Among these books, the one on Kashmir, titled *Kashmir: Paradise in Turmoil,* published in 1994, was most successful. Its first edition got sold out at a book fair in Delhi soon after publication. He later published a revised second edition of the book. In 1996, he also brought out a thoroughly revised second edition of his first book, *Rajasthan ka Itihas.*

Father completed his autobiography titled *My Little World* in 1999. In its preface, he makes the interesting observation that after authoring seven other books on history and economics in both Hindi and English, he had discovered that writing one's autobiography was the most difficult task. It took him three years to pen the book. And yet he must have not been fully satisfied with it, since he chose not to publish it. Instead, he got his sister's son, who ran a printing press in Bhilwara, to print about a hundred copies of it for circulation within the family. It is thanks to this gem that I have now been able to write the present biography.

After the autobiography, Father wrote one last book but it remained unpublished while he lived. The book comprehensively covered all chief ministers of Rajasthan and was completed in early 2001. It is likely that Father was not fully satisfied with the manuscript. Ravi recently got it published by a local publisher posthumously.

While writing these books, Father also continued to write articles for both local and, at a lesser frequency, national newspapers, such as the *Hindustan Times, Times of India* and *Economic Times*. His articles on the state's economy and budgets attracted the attention of the local elite and the electronic media. The result was that he became a permanent fixture on the local lecture circuit, which included Rotary and Lions Clubs, Federation of Indian Chamber of Commerce and Industry (FICCI), Rajasthan Chamber of Commerce and Industry, and University of Rajasthan. He became associated with the Rajasthan Economic Association and served for several years on FICCI's taxation committee. Around budget time, he offered his commentary on local radio and television.

While engaged in these activities, Father also took up causes that he saw as important for the state of Rajasthan. Two such causes, in which he got deeply involved and made a difference, are worthy of a close look. I devote the remainder of this chapter to their detailed discussion. The first of them concerns economics, and the second, history.

India is a federation in which some functions are assigned exclusively to the central government (for example, telecommunications, defence and foreign policy), some exclusively to state governments (law and order, electricity distribution) and some to both (education, health, infrastructure). To perform these functions, the Centre and states need revenues. Taxes constitute the largest source of revenue. Keeping the efficiency of tax collection in view, the manner in which the Constitution divides the powers of taxation creates an imbalance between revenues and expenditures. Specifically, under the Constitution, the Centre gets to collect a disproportionately large proportion of the nation's total tax revenues. This creates a shortfall of revenues in the states.

Given this imbalance, the Constitution provides for the sharing of tax revenues raised by the Centre between it and the states. The tax kitty that must be shared between the two levels of administration is called the 'divisible pool'. What the share of states in this pool of resources is, and how this share is to be parcelled among different states, are big questions, not just economically but also politically.

Accordingly, the Constitution provides for the appointment of an independent Finance Commission every five years to recommend how the divisible pool should be shared between the Centre and states (vertical distribution) and how the states' share should be apportioned among the states (horizontal distribution). In apportioning each state its share, the Finance Commission is expected to favour the poorer states over the richer ones. The rationale for this is that poorer states are less capable of raising their own tax revenues and need extra resources to bridge the gap between them and the richer states in terms of infrastructure, education and health. Because of the extreme sensitivity of states as to the matter of receiving their 'fair' share of revenues, successive Finance Commissions clearly spell out the formulas they use to determine the proportion of each state's share in the divisible pool.

Two years after my father's retirement from government service, the Seventh Finance Commission delivered its report in October 1978. Now that he had the luxury of time, which he lacked earlier, Father decided to study the report carefully from the viewpoint of the state of Rajasthan. He noticed that the share of the state in the tax revenue pie to be apportioned among states, as recommended by the Seventh Finance Commission, had fallen significantly relative to that recommended by the Sixth Finance Commission. On closer examination, he found that the key factor behind this fall was the inclusion of a set of poverty estimates as one of the criteria for inter se distribution of tax revenues.

The Finance Commission had rightly chosen to base the division partially on poverty levels, such that the poorer a state, the larger would be its share of revenues. But the poverty estimates it used were seriously flawed. They showed that states such as Maharashtra and Gujarat had proportionately more poor people than Rajasthan did. This made little sense. Per-capita net state domestic product (NSDP) estimates at current prices in the year 1980–81 placed Rajasthan in the fourteenth place among the existing fifteen large states at the time. Only Bihar had lower per-capita NSDP than Rajasthan that year. Maharashtra and Gujarat ranked second and fourth, respectively, in per capita NSDP ranking.

Separately, based on his experience of working in the state government, Father was acutely aware that bringing roads, electricity and water to the people was a far more serious challenge in a sparsely populated state such as Rajasthan than in densely populated states. Innumerable small habitations were spread across the vast desert land of the state. Yet, successive Finance Commissions had taken into account only the population, but not land area, among its criteria for inter se distribution of tax revenues to the states. Nor had the Rajasthan state government made a plea to any of the past Finance Commissions for the inclusion of land area as one of the criteria in their representations. Father conveyed these points to the state government so that it could represent the state's interests better the next time around.

Less than four years later, in June 1982, the central government appointed the Eighth Finance Commission. This time around, my father was prepared. Early in the Commission's term, he submitted a memorandum to it arguing that it refrain from using the poverty estimates that the Seventh Finance Commission had used, and that the land area of the state be included, alongside population, in the criteria for determining the horizontal division of the states' shares in the divisible pool. Later, when the Commission came for consultation to Jaipur, the state capital, it invited my father to offer his thoughts. Father went before the Commission and made his case in the strongest terms he could. He later recalled that when he bluntly criticized the poverty estimates used by the Seventh Finance Commission, chairman of the commission, Y.B. Chavan, was visibly annoyed.

Apparently, the poverty estimates the Commission was using were derived from a formula that heavily depended on calorie consumption. Anyone with calorie consumption above a specified threshold was classified as non-poor. At the time, due to poverty, there was a disproportionate consumption of millets by the rural folk in Rajasthan. Millets were cheaper than finer grains such as wheat and rice. Millets were also high in calorie content. Therefore, paradoxically, the poverty-forced choice of coarse grains in the state resulted in lower levels of measured poverty in Rajasthan. To make his point forcefully, Father went on to tell the Commission that during times of drought many people in rural Rajasthan end up consuming a particular grass, which is richer in calorie content than even millets. If calories consumed from that grass were included in the calculations, poverty levels in Rajasthan would turn out to be lower still! That line of argument left Chavan quite exasperated.

Father came out of the meeting quite certain that he had lost the battle. But when the Eighth Finance Commission submitted its report, he was pleasantly surprised that it had dropped the disputed poverty estimates in deciding upon inter se distribution of the states' share in the divisible pool. Judging by the press articles that my father saw coming out around the time that the

Commission was doing its work, he was the only person to have argued against the poverty estimates unequivocally. As such he was doubly pleased; at a personal level, it was a victory for him, but it was also something that helped the state.

In 1988, the central government appointed the Ninth Finance Commission under the chairmanship of N.K.P. Salve. It was charged with giving its first report for 1989–90 and a second and final report for the years 1990–91 to 1994–95. The reason for this unusual charge was that the government wanted to align the tax devolution years of the Finance Commission with the Five-Year Plans. Much to my father's dismay, the report for the year 1989–90 by the Ninth Finance Commission resurrected the calorie consumption-based estimates of poverty, against which he had fought with the Eighth Finance Commission.

Therefore, when the Commission came to Jaipur for consultation with the state for its second and final report, my father sought a meeting with it as a private citizen representing the interests of the state. As per the tradition, the Commission accepted his request. Father argued with Salve for nearly an hour to drive home why it was a mistake to use the said poverty estimates in determining inter se distribution of the states' shares in divisible pool. Frustrated, Salve told my father that the chief minister of the state had already agreed to the use of those very estimates. Father replied that he spoke only on his own behalf as a concerned citizen of the state. As with the Eighth Finance Commission, my father left the meeting convinced that he had failed to persuade the Commission members. But, once again, when the Commission's recommendations came out, it was good news for him and his state; the Commission had dropped the use of calorie consumption-based poverty estimates.

My father's final victory on behalf of the state of Rajasthan in the battle for securing a fairer share for his state came with the Tenth Finance Commission. He had argued with the two previous Commissions for inclusion of land area alongside population to determine inter se distribution of the states' shares in the divisible pool, but had not succeeded. The Tenth Finance Commission, chaired by K.C. Pant, finally included land area among the criteria in its recommendations on inter se distribution of tax revenues.

The battle for the second cause my father decided to take up was fought a lot more publicly. This one was in the realm of history and proved a lot more controversial than any other he had fought in his public life. The question was about the place of Maharana Pratap – revered no less by the people of Rajasthan than Shivaji by the people of Maharashtra – in the history of India. Because of the intellectual value of the debate on the key question and the controversial nature of what my father championed, the episode requires a detailed discussion, beginning with a brief consideration of the relevant history.

Babur, the ruler of Kabul, laid the foundation of Mughal rule in India in 1526 CE. That year, he defeated Sultan Ibrahim Lodi in the famous First Battle of Panipat. At this time, Rajputana was ruled by a Rajput confederacy led by Rana Sanga. Sanga himself wanted to end the Muslim rule in Delhi and replace it with Rajput rule. To this end, originally, he had offered to join Babur in his assault on Ibrahim Lodi, in the hope that after scoring a victory, Babur would return to Kabul and he would become the ruler of Delhi. But he found out that Babur's plan was to stay as the ruler of Delhi and therefore decided not to assist him. But once Babur won Delhi, Sanga was ready to take him head on and establish Rajput rule in Delhi. Accordingly, he challenged Babur and fought a fierce battle against him in Khanwa in 1527. But two of his key Rajput clansmen sabotaged him; they, with their armies, joined hands with the enemy. Sanga lost the battle.

Akbar, grandson of Babur and son of Humayun, ascended the throne in Delhi in 1556. He was an ambitious ruler who wanted to bring much of India under his rule. Though the Kachhawa ruler of Amber (near Jaipur, which was not yet founded) had surrendered to him in 1562, other major Rajput kingdoms, such as Bikaner, Jodhpur, Jaisalmer and Mewar, had shown no inclination to do the same. Akbar knew that the key to bringing the Rajput kingdoms under his suzerainty was the defeat of Maharana Udai Singh, third son of Rana Sanga, who had come to occupy the throne of Mewar in 1537 . To that end, he himself led an expedition to the fort of Chittor in 1567.

Though Udai Singh had already left Chittor and disappeared into the hills by the time Akbar arrived there, the latter pressed ahead in the hope that a victory in this battle would break the resolve of the Rajput kings of many other states. For four months, he persevered in his effort to bring down the gates and walls of the fort, but was unsuccessful. But in the end, the defending soldiers and their families inside the fort ran out of food and other supplies. Outnumbered but unwilling to surrender, they took the only recourse they knew: the womenfolk and children threw themselves into the fire, thus committing Jauhar, and the menfolk put on soldiers' attire and went out to fight until death. Akbar finally scored a victory over Chittor in February 1568 and, contrary to the local tradition that forbade the victor from punishing civilians, went on to massacre 20,000 innocent souls.

Just as Akbar had hoped, the fall of Chittor led the rulers of Jodhpur, Bikaner, Jaisalmer and Hadoti to surrender to the

Mughals. But Udai Singh refused to accept his suzerainty. Indeed, once Akbar had left Mewar, he returned from the hills and founded a new capital one hundred kilometres west and south of Chittor, which came to be known as Udaipur. Unfortunately, before the construction of Udaipur was completed, Udai Singh died.

Upon the death of Udai Singh, his brave son Pratap succeeded him in 1572. During this and the following year, Akbar sent as many as four emissaries to persuade Pratap to accept his suzerainty. Pratap received each with due courtesy but refused to oblige Akbar. Frustrated, Akbar sent an expedition against Pratap under Man Singh, grandson of the then king of Amber. The two armies met and clashed in Haldighati in 1576. Pratap was defeated and wounded, but his legendary horse Chetak managed to carry him out of the battlefield and beyond the reach of the enemy. After this battle, he concluded that he did not stand a chance against the mighty army of Akbar in a direct battle. Therefore, he changed tactics and switched to guerilla warfare. For the following thirteen years, Pratap remained invisible to the Mughal army but kept it on tenterhooks. He moved from one place to another with his family, and despite innumerable hardships refused to accept Mughal suzerainty.

Akbar sent armies in 1580 and 1584 to Mewar, but they were unsuccessful in capturing Pratap. But after 1585, Akbar decided not to pursue the latter any more and diverted his attention to conquests in and consolidation of other parts of India. Because Pratap was popular with the people and the local tribes were committed to his cause, by 1587 he was able to recover all his territories except Chittor and Mandalgarh. He spent the following twelve years rebuilding Mewar, which he successfully did, with prosperity returning to the region. During this period, he also completed the construction of the city of Udaipur. He died in 1597.

In the hearts and minds of the people of Rajasthan, especially of Mewar, Pratap is a rare patriot and revered hero. Whereas one by one all the Rajput rulers of his time became vassels of Akbar, he refused to submit to him. For those like my father from the region, who felt passionate about the freedom struggle against the British, Pratap was a great source of inspiration. Inaugurating the state of Rajasthan, even Sardar Patel gave a great tribute to Pratap, telling the audience that the new state represented the realization of his dream. Statues of Pratap can be found in nearly all parts of not just Rajasthan but in entire India. His birth anniversary is celebrated throughout the country. It is also a public holiday in the states of Rajasthan, Haryana and Himachal Pradesh.

Nevertheless, while historians largely applaud Pratap for his valour, some of them also hold the view that he was an obstacle to the unification of India and that he was responsible for keeping his people backward longer than was necessary. I have found the earliest expression of this view in the PhD thesis of historian Gopi Nath Sharma, written under the supervision of the leading historian of the time, A.L. Srivastava, at the University of Agra in 1951. Dr Sharma published the thesis in 1954 under the title *Mewar and the Mughal Emperors*. I am not a historian, either by training or practice, but as a researcher and scholar in the field of economics, I find the book an excellent piece of work. It is based on extensive original research and is lucid in its narrative.

At the time the first edition of the book came out, Dr Sharma was a faculty member in the Department of History at Maharana Bhupal College in Udaipur, where my father had done his own high school in 1938. Later, by the time I went to college in 1967, he had moved to the University of Rajasthan. I studied at Rajasthan College, which was an integral part of the University of Rajasthan. As history was one of my electives in my BA course, I had the privilege of taking a few classes with Dr Sharma. He was the best history teacher I had.

In *Mewar and the Mughal Emperors*, Dr Sharma has the highest praise for Pratap. For instance, evaluating him at the end of the chapter titled 'Pratap and Akbar', he writes:

> As regards Pratap, it must be said that for twenty-five years he had played an important part upon the political stage, and represented with remarkable fidelity the views of the great majority of his subjects. He was a great ruler by virtue of his being a good man, with homely virtue, simple life, dauntless courage, untiring industry, generosity, and kindness which won him general affection and respect.[9]

Dr Sharma goes on to add:

> Pratap's death did more than close an epoch. It removed from the stage of Rajput politics its most attractive and most striking personality… As an optimist he took all the blows of adverse fortune with equanimity, and he never bore a grudge against it. By his spirit and success, the soldiers were taught to act, the subjects to hope, and the enemies to fear and respect.[10]

---

9 G.N. Sharma, *Mewar and the Mughal Emperors*, Agra: Shiva Lal Agarwala &Co. Ltd, 1954, pp.119-20

10 Ibid., p. 120

The chapter closes with this glowing tribute:

> He upheld the pride of the Hindus and as long as this race lives, it will cherish with pride the memory of one who had staked his all in a fight against an alien. As a great warrior of liberty, a devoted lover of noble cause and a hero of moral character, his name is to millions of men even today, a cloud of hope by day and a pillar of fire by night.[11]

There is thus ample evidence that Dr Sharma has the utmost admiration for Pratap. He also recognizes and appreciates the highest respect and deep love that the people of Rajasthan, especially of Mewar, have for him. Nevertheless, in the last paragraph of the chapter just before his concluding sentences above, he writes, about Pratap:

> Great as he was, one might speculate whether the struggle tended to contribute to the welfare of the country as a whole or produced adverse effect on the future of the land. It is to be admitted as Akbar was a great and benevolent sovereign who pursued the grand policy of unifying the country both politically and culturally, Pratap's remaining aloof from the union was a great impediment in that noble task. To that extent it was injurious to the interest of his country. If at this stage Pratap would have joined the Mughal order, he could have saved his country from disaster and ruin. Even his long resistance could not avert the days when during his own son's time Mewar became a subordinate state of the Mughal empire. Had this opportunity

---

11 Ibid., p. 121

> been given to Mewar earlier much of its backwardness could have been mended.[12]

This is an extremely serious indictment of Pratap, and I shall come to its careful dissection below. Presently, let me note that the thesis that Pratap was an obstacle to national unity also finds expression in the 1957 book *Akbar* by the great scholar Rahul Sankrityayan. Going by the sources he cites in Appendix 5 of the book, it would seem that he was unaware of the book by Dr Sharma. Therefore, one can plausibly take the view that he came to this conclusion independently. According to my father, several influential historians of post-Independence India, such as Romila Thapar, Bipin Chandra and Barun De, also subscribe to this thesis.

In the preface to the book, Sankrityayan states that after the great King Ashoka, who ruled in the third century BCE, Akbar was the only lodestar to appear on the horizon of India. He characterizes Akbar as a patriot in the true sense of the term, and as one who took the nation to new heights. Sankrityayan devotes approximately two pages to the struggle between Akbar and Pratap. He has much praise for Pratap in these two succinct pages. But he also criticizes him as someone who believed in a fragmented rather than unified India. He expresses this view in these words:

> We should not forget that if Pratap was a warrior willing to sacrifice his life to defend the honour of his family and dharma on the one hand, he represented the school of thought that believed

12 Ibid., p. 121

in the vivisection of the nation into hundreds of pieces on the other.[13] (Translated from the Hindi by Arvind Panagariya.)

It is not difficult to take issue with the thesis that Pratap belonged to a school that believed in the division of India into small bits and with the related propositions around it by Dr Sharma and Sankrityayan. If India were to be unified under a single ruler, surely the latter did not necessarily have to be an alien one. In principle, why could Pratap not have been that ruler? Indeed, that was the ambition that had led his grandfather Rana Sanga to first ditch Babur in his battle against Ibrahim Lodi and then challenge him directly in Khanwa. He wanted to wrest the throne of Delhi for himself, from where he could have unified India. It simply turned out that two of his key confederates broke away from him with their armies and joined the enemy. Consequently, he lost the decisive battle to Babur.

By the time Pratap came on the scene, the Mughals had become considerably stronger. But from his viewpoint, Akbar was the grandson of an invader, with whom his grandfather had fought the final battle before the establishment of Mughal rule in Delhi. How could fighting against such a ruler be anything but an act of patriotism for him? Indeed, in his final tribute to Pratap quoted above, Dr Sharma himself characterizes Akbar as an alien when he says that Pratap 'staked his all in a fight against an alien'.

Pratap could also not forget that his father Udai Singh's resistance to Akbar had been an inspiration to the Rajput rulers of Jodhpur, Bikaner, Jaisalmer and Hadoti. It was only after Chittor fell to Akbar that these rulers lost their nerve and accepted his

---

13 Rahul Sankrityayan, *Akbar*, Kitab Mahal, 1957, p. 221

suzerainty. True, the Kachhawa king of Jaipur, Bharmal, had submitted to Mughal authority and had given his daughter in marriage to Akbar well before the fall of Chittor in 1562. But can we conclude that by doing so he was helping Akbar build a unified India? Such a suggestion would be laughable, in view of the fact that Bharmal's decision was nothing more than surrender. At the time he submitted to Akbar's authority, enemies from within posed existential threat to him. By accepting Akbar's suzerainty and giving him his daughter in marriage, he had 'bought' imperial protection against these enemies.

Dr Sharma argues that Akbar was 'a great and benevolent sovereign' on a mission to foster political and cultural unity among Indians.[14] Sankrityayan expresses very similar sentiments in the preface to his book. While this may have been true of Akbar during the latter part of his reign, it was hardly the case during the active phase of his campaign against Mewar. Only four years before Pratap ascended the throne, Akbar had mercilessly killed 20,000 innocent civilians following the fall of Chittor. Surely, Pratap could not have viewed him as a benevolent ruler.

An incident that Sankrityayan quotes in *Akbar* graphically illustrates that the Mughal attitude towards the local people had remained unchanged even eight years after the fall of Chittor, when Pratap fought the battle of Haldighati. The episode is a reminder that Akbar's Muslim generals continued to view non-Muslim lives, including those of Rajputs on their own side, with disdain. In the battle, Pratap was pitched against a force led by Rajput Prince Man Singh of Amber. Asaf Khan, another general of equal rank in Akbar's army, had accompanied Man Singh.

---

14 Sharma, *Mewar and the Mughal Emperors*, 1954, p. 121

Historian Abdul Qadir Badayuni was serving under him in this battle. According to Sankrityayan, at one point, Badayuni asked Asaf Khan, 'In this intense battle, how do you distinguish between Rajput warriors on our side and those on the enemy side?' Asaf Khan replied, 'Regardless of which side they are on, when Rajput soldiers fall, Islam benefits.'[15]

It is true that Akbar was by far the most tolerant of the Mughal rulers and that he genuinely worked towards promoting cultural harmony in the latter part of his reign. But it is also true that Hindus were far from equal partners in this project. When he married the daughter of the Jaipur king Bharmal, she had to convert to Islam and assume a Muslim name. The same was the case with the granddaughter of Bharmal who was married to Akbar's son Salim (later known as Jahangir) from Bharmal's daughter. One may speculate that the marriage of the aunt and niece to a father-son pair was in violation of the Rajput tradition and practice. It is doubtful that Rajput tradition would approve of a Rajput prince marrying his maternal uncle's daughter. Yet, that is exactly what Bharmal's granddaughter was to Salim. Finally, we may ask why this cultural harmony flowed only one way, with the hand of Rajput princesses being asked in marriage for Mughal royals but Mughal princesses never offered to Rajput royals? True cultural harmony and equality would require two-way marital relationships.

Dr Sharma also hypothesizes that had Pratap accepted the suzerainty of Akbar during his time, 'much of its [Mewar's]

---

15 Sankrityayan, *Akbar*, 1957, p. 223

backwardness could have been mended'.[16] This too is an assertion unsupported by evidence. Chittor and Mandalgarh had fallen to the Mughals even before Pratap had ascended the throne and remained under their control throughout his life. Did they become more prosperous than the part of Mewar that remained under the control of Pratap? Dr Sharma makes no attempt to answer this question. Going by the descriptions of prosperity that Pratap brought to the part of Mewar that remained under him during the last twelve years of his peaceful rule, an affirmative answer to the question is by no means a foregone conclusion.

In the course of writing his own history books, my father had reviewed the writings of many historians, including Dr Sharma and Sankrityayan. Coming from the Mewar region and having closely worked with Mewar Praja Mandal, Father had a particular interest in and deep admiration for Pratap. Therefore, the thesis that by taking on to Akbar, Pratap had turned into an obstacle to national unity, deeply troubled him. In a long footnote in the preface to his 1982 book *Rajasthan ka Itihas*, Father expressed his discomfort in these strong words:

> In the name of secularism and cultural unity, certain modern historians including Rahul Sankrityayan, Romila Thapar and Dr Gopinath Sharma have characterized the opposition of Rana Pratap to Akbar as unnatural or a barrier to national unity. The learned authors forgot that Pratap considered Akbar a foreign invader. How could he forget that only 50 years earlier, Babur, the ruler of Fergana principality of Afghanistan, had become the ruler

16 Sharma, *Mewar and the Mughal Emperors*, 1954, p. 121

> of Delhi after first defeating Ibrahim Lodi and then his [Pratap's] very own grandfather Rana Sanga? At the time, acceptance of Babur's grandson Akbar as the ruler of India by Pratap or any other Indian ruler for that matter was not only impossible but also unnatural. In fact, the occasion to accept Mughals as Indian rulers arose only 260 years after the death of Pratap, when Hindus and Muslims fought shoulder to shoulder against the British under the leadership of the last Mughal emperor Bahadur Shah Zafar in 1857.[17]

Father felt that if, after 150 years of British rule, his own generation still treated the British as foreign rulers, how could Pratap and his contemporaries accept Mughals as Indian rulers just fifty years after they had arrived? Seen this way, it was the duty of Pratap and all other rulers of India to challenge Mughals. It was akin to the duty of his generation to fight against the British.

Because Dr Sharma was in Jaipur, my father personally shared his objections with him. Dr Sharma assured him that he would delete the paragraphs in question when a new edition of his book came out. While a new edition of *Mewar and the Mughal Emperors* was perhaps still in the making, a new printing of another of Dr Sharma's books, *Rajasthan ka Itihas* (History of Rajasthan), came out in 1989. Originally published in 1971, this book was a prescribed text for one of the history courses at the University of Rajasthan. In its 1989 edition, Dr Sharma had stuck to his thesis on Pratap, as advanced in *Mewar and the Mughal Emperors*.

---

17 B.L. Panagariya, *Rajasthan ka Itihas*, 1982, p. ix

In *Rajasthan ka Itihas*, Dr Sharma had covered all the major princely states that eventually came to constitute Rajasthan. They included Amber-Jaipur, which had accepted the suzerainty of Akbar as early as 1562, giving him one of its princesses in marriage. Dr Sharma describes these acts of Bharmal, the ruler of Amber at the time, as evidence of 'farsightedness' and 'diplomacy'. According to him, Bharmal inspired other Rajput kings to give their daughters in marriage to Mughal royals too, which promoted harmony between Muslims and Hindus. Because Akbar permitted the Rajput princesses to observe Hindu festivals and rituals after they joined the Mughal household, the marriages contributed to cultural harmony between Muslims and Hindus.

My father saw these marriages quite differently. For him, Bharmal's acceptance of Akbar's suzerainty at the time was no different from the submission by rulers of princely states to British authority. In both cases, subservience to the superior power allowed the local rulers to perpetuate their rule on a hereditary basis without being challenged by their people, no matter how poorly they governed.

On the specific claim by Dr Sharma of promotion of Hindu-Muslim harmony through the marriages of Rajput princesses to Mughal royals, one must look beyond the fact of celebration of Hindu festivals with their accompanying rituals and ask whether it gave rise to a more tolerant generation of Mughal rulers subsequently. There is no evidence that it did. Indeed, Akbar's grandson Aurangzeb turned out to be a far less tolerant ruler than Akbar. He forcibly converted Hindus to Islam, destroyed numerous Hindu temples and reintroduced jizya, a tax applicable only to non-Muslims. In *The Oxford History of India*, Vincent

Smith writes that in 1669, Aurangzeb ordered all the governors of his provinces to 'destroy with a willing hand the schools and temples of the infidels, and that they were strictly enjoined to put an entire stop to the teaching and practice of idolatrous forms of worship'.[18]

At an intellectual level, my father had no reservations about authors holding views divergent from his own. He was well aware of the millennia-long Indian tradition in this respect. What bothered him was that the book *Rajasthan ka Itihas* by Dr Sharma was a prescribed text in the curriculum of the University of Rajasthan. He felt that students should not be given a one-sided view on a subject, especially when it happens to deal with a question of great local sensitivity. Alongside, they must be exposed to the counterview. Since he felt strongly about the matter, he decided to raise it publicly at an appropriate opportunity.

That opportunity came in June 1992. Because of his regular writings in *Rajasthan Patrika*, various organizations in Jaipur used to invite Father to speak on the subjects of Rajasthan's economy, finance and history. One of them was the Rajasthan Chhatra Vikas Sangthan, a senior student organization. It invited him as the principal speaker at an event at the university to celebrate the 452nd birth anniversary of Maharana Pratap on 4 June 1992. Dr Rameshwar Sharma, the vice chancellor of the University of Rajasthan, was to preside over the event. Father decided to bring the matter up in his speech.

At the event, Father spoke eloquently for an hour of Pratap's valour as he fought against an alien ruler for more than a decade,

---

18 Vincent Arthur Smith, *The Oxford History of India From the Earliest Times to the End of 1911*, Oxford: Clarendon Press, 1919, p. 437

refusing to compromise on his freedom. He said that any nation, big or small, would be proud of a patriot and a hero like him. He then went on to add that despite this, Pratap was being denigrated in his own land in the books prescribed for students of the University of Rajasthan. There were cries of 'shame' from the audience. Later, when the vice chancellor spoke, he assured the audience that the university would look into the matter.

The next morning, one of the local newspapers, *Rashtradoot*, whose correspondent had been present at the event, published a six-column front-page story with the sensational title 'Maharana Pratap Considered a Traitor in the University Curriculum'. The story called for removal of the controversial book from the curriculum. Soon the subject assumed national importance, with the *Hindustan Times*, *Times of India*, *Indian Express* and other dailies and weeklies publishing Father's interviews alongside those supporting Dr Sharma's views. All India Radio and BBC also broadcast my father's interviews. In his interviews and in an op-ed piece published in the *Hindustan Times*, Father made it clear that his stand was not against the book but against it being prescribed in the university curriculum.

The academic council of the University of Rajasthan met on 20 August 1992 and decided to suspend the teaching of *Rajasthan ka Itihas* by Dr Sharma. Writing on the episode in a 1997 book titled *The Book on Trial: Fundamentalism and Censorship in India*, Girija Kumar writes that there was 'outside' pressure and that the vice chancellor was 'in an unseemly hurry to comply with political pressure'.[19] Kumar does not explain the source of this

---

19 Girija Kumar, *The Book on Trial: Fundamentalism and Censorship in India*, New Delhi: Har-Anand Publications, 1997, p. 429

political pressure, but we may speculate that he is pointing a finger at the Bhairon Singh Shekhawat-led Bharatiya Janata Party (BJP) government, which happened to be at the helm at the time. Since my father was well known to be a lifelong supporter of the Congress, he would certainly not have had any personal clout with a BJP government. But the cause of defending the honour of Pratap may have resonated with the BJP leadership, leading it to press the university administration to drop the book from the curriculum. This is a plausible hypothesis but, as we will see shortly, not a compelling one.

In his account of the episode, Kumar does not mention that far more overt political pressure came from the opposite side. Governor Channa Reddy, who served at the pleasure of the Congress-led central government and was ex-officio chancellor of the university, summarily suspended Vice Chancellor Rameshwar Sharma, alleging multiple wrongdoings on his part. A single-member commission headed by Justice Shrimal, a former chief justice of the Sikkim High Court, was appointed to look into the matter.

The key allegation against vice chancellor Rameshwar Sharma was that he had wrongfully removed Dr Gopinath Sharma's book from the curriculum. My father was naturally called to testify on the matter. A lawyer of the commission began by asking my father how he could call himself a historian when he neither had a doctorate in the subject nor had taught the subject at any recognized institution. Father politely replied that the learned lawyer was correct in noting his lack of qualifications as a historian and that he had never claimed to be one. He went on to remind him, however, that the greatest historians of Rajasthan had come not from the ranks of scholars in the universities but from the administration. In support of his point, he cited the names of such stalwarts on the history of Rajasthan as Muhnot Nainsi, James Tod, Shyamaldas and Gaurishankar Hirachand Ojha. He then went on to quote extracts from Dr Gopinath Sharma's book relating to Pratap and explained why the academic council and the vice chancellor had been right in their decision. From the final outcome, it would seem that my father was successful in persuading the commission to his point of view. It completely exonerated the vice chancellor, with the university reinstating him soon after.

Echoes of my father's battle in Rajasthan were later heard as far as the Rajya Sabha. In March 1993, the Upper House debated the appropriateness of the inclusion of books that contained disparaging remarks on national heroes such as Pratap, Shivaji and Guru Nanak in school, college and university curriculums. Cutting across party lines, the Upper House overwhelmingly came out against such a practice. The presiding officer directed the Government of India to ensure that such books were dropped from course syllabuses.

The postscript to the story, as reported by Kumar, however, is that the university reinstated Dr Gopinath Sharma's book in May 1996. At the time, the same BJP chief minister – Bhairon Singh Shekhawat – was at the helm. Though the Narasimha Rao government had dismissed BJP-led governments in nearly all states in the wake of the Babri Masjid demolition, the elections that were held a year later in December 1993 had returned Shekhawat to office. This fact casts doubts on the validity of the hypothesis that pressure by him or his government had been behind the original withdrawal of the book from the curriculum. Kumar himself credits academic historians, who stood solidly behind Dr Sharma, for restoration of the status quo ante.

Controversies similar to the one on the role of Pratap in Mewar have played out multiple times on the role of Shivaji in Maharashtra. Kumar reviews them in careful detail in his book. Based on his account, I conclude this chapter with one such controversy, which involved a figure no less than India's first prime minister, Pandit Jawaharlal Nehru.

In the first edition of *Glimpses of the World History*, published in 1934, Nehru had made some disparaging remarks on Shivaji. He wrote,

> With his enemies he [Shivaji] was prepared to adopt any means, good or bad, provided that he gained his end. He killed a general sent against him by Bijapur by treachery.' Nehru went on to add, 'Some of Shivaji's deeds, like the treacherous killing of the Bijapur general, lower him greatly in estimation.'[20]

Pune political and intellectual circles took serious exception to these remarks denigrating the great hero of Maharashtra. Congress leader T.R. Deogirikar conveyed the depth of the resentment in these circles to Nehru in a letter. In his reply, Nehru was quick to accept his mistake and stated that he was pleased to be corrected. He dropped the offending reference from the next and subsequent editions of *Glimpses of the World History*. Public figures are clearly much more sensitive to public sentiment than academics. The two indeed have very different objectives and constituencies.

20 As quoted by Girja Kumar, *The Book on Trial: Fundamentalism and Censorship in India*, Delhi: Har-Anand Publications, 1997, p. 431

8

Reflections on a Father Extraordinaire

IN HIS LIFE, MY father took on numerous public causes, both inside as well as outside the government. He did what he thought was right, with passion and courage, giving the causes his all. At the same time, he did not neglect his duty towards us, the children. During our formative years, he remained attentive to the long-term direction of our careers while also monitoring our progress on an almost daily basis. The only thing he compromised on was his own career.

He chose to stay with the Rajasthan Secretariat Services so that his posting would remain fixed in Jaipur during the critical years of our education. He knew that his income was far too meagre to send any of us to residential schools in any of the major cities in India. Therefore, returning to politics or availing of opportunities such as joining the RAS, which could have led to faster promotions but would have also required movement from one place to another, would have compromised our studies. Indeed, even in Jaipur he could not afford to send us to the elite English-medium schools such as St. Xavier High School. That meant that he had to work extra hard on us at home for our success.

Not having gone to school, my mother could not read or write. Therefore, she could not directly aid us in our studies or otherwise assess our academic progress. But she was an active participant in monitoring and disciplining us. A day would rarely pass without her scolding us for not having spent enough time on our lessons. She was fundamentally an intelligent woman and would remind us daily to do our homework. She kept track of our examinations, ensuring that we could study undisturbed and uninterrupted when preparing for them.

Mother handled the family finances and, despite having had no formal education, never made a mistake in tracking them. She could give a complete item-by-item account of monthly expenditures from memory. One of her major strengths was that throughout our lives, she managed the family budget within Father's income without complaining that she did not have enough funds to meet the necessary monthly expenditures. Father would hand over to her a fixed sum at the beginning of each month, and she would finance all expenditures out of it. She worked hard to manage the household, keeping order in the family. Until I left India in 1974, she would make the special dishes, desserts and snacks for all festivals at home to economize on expenses. Treats for Diwali – all kinds of papris and shakkarparas – would be made to last throughout the vacation period, and we loved them.

When it came to many traditional dishes from Mewar, she had a magical hand.

As a devout Jain, Mother went on a lot of fasts, especially during the eight-day annual holy event of Paryushana. On the concluding day of the event, Samvatsari, all Jains are encouraged to fast, staying on water only. But the days immediately preceding and following this day are celebrated with numerous traditional homemade dishes. On the preceding day, you prepare yourself for the fasting day, and on the following day you are rewarded for having fasted! For Mother, Samvatsari would often be the third day of continuous fasting, but she would get up at 4 a.m. the following day to get an early start on cooking the fancy dishes we had come to expect of her.

According to traditional belief, fasting cleanses your soul, and therefore the day following Samvatsari is celebrated as a day on which to seek forgiveness from all for any hurt you may have caused them the preceding year. We could never forget this because when we woke up on the morning after Samvatsari and went to pay our respects to Mother in the kitchen, the first thing she would do was to seek our forgiveness for any hurt she had caused us. We would then reciprocate and begin our own routine of seeking forgiveness from all others we knew.

While Mother could not read and write, she had excellent skills of comprehension. She, obviously, had no knowledge of English. But in the 1980s and 1990s, when we would come to visit the family from the United States during summer vacations, I would often observe my nieces (Ravi's and Ashok's daughters) watching the afternoon shows in English on television. My mother, who would be sitting in the room too, could more or less follow the storyline without any understanding of the dialogue. Even more interestingly, when she and Father visited us in the United States in 1985, sometimes it was she who would be explaining to him the television shows. The American accent, which Father found difficult to follow, had robbed him of the advantage of knowing English when it came to watching these shows.

Though Father rarely expressed it, he was aware and appreciative of the importance of my mother in his life and in the smooth running of the family affairs. When the two of them differed on an important family issue, most of the time it was Mother who prevailed. His own dependence on her naturally grew as they advanced in age. For me, it was a pleasant surprise to see Father's generous acknowledgement of Mother's importance in his life in his autobiography. In the section devoted to his personal life, he wrote,

> We have completed 65 years of married life in June 1999. For us the journey from Suwana to Jaipur was not an easy one. We have seen many ups and downs during our long journey but went through them cheerfully. My wife was always a source of strength to me even in the most trying circumstances. It was due to her that I could maintain high standards of integrity throughout my life.[21]

I do not know if my father also conveyed these thoughts to my mother. Since she had no ability to read even Hindi, let alone English, I very much hope that he did.

The fact that the family could own a house and a car while also meeting its daily needs on Father's meagre salary speaks volumes

21 Panagariya, *My Little World.*

about my parents' frugal living style and Father's excellent long-term financial planning. One of the luckiest or perhaps most farsighted things that Father did was to build a house of his own as early as the late 1950s. One of my earliest memories is of Father occasionally returning from his morning walks with a rose or two, over which we siblings used to fight. We were living in a first-floor rented flat in a building on M. I. Road in those days, and I used to tell Father to build a bungalow of our own one day and grow roses in it. That dream came true sooner than I could have imagined.

To buy land and build the house, Father had to take a loan from the government. But his salary placed a relatively low ceiling on even the loan amount for which he qualified. The amount had to be such that after deduction of the monthly instalment to repay the loan in a few years, the net take-home salary was sufficient to meet the day-to-day family expenses. With the limited loan, the only location where he could afford to buy land was way outside the city, in what seemed to be a jungle at the time. When the house was built and we moved there in 1959, there were no other houses on either side of it as far as one could see. There was a mazaar and a burial ground across from the house and a famous Ganesh temple some 200 yards away, but nothing else. At the back of the house there were a few huts made of mud and straw. The result was that the land price Father paid was less than Re 1 per square yard.

Within one to two years after we arrived, there was a burglary in the house. There were easily a dozen people sleeping in various parts of the house that day, but the thieves were real professionals. They chose a time in the night when everyone was in deep sleep. They took whatever little jewellery my mother and my recently married sister Premlata had, but nothing else. Within a day's time, they had melted the jewellery and sold the gold they had extracted from it. The total value of the theft, ranging between Rs 4,000 and Rs 5,000 at the time, may not seem much today, but was a serious blow to the financial security of the family. Eventually, the thieves were caught, but only a fraction of the loss was recovered.

The episode left a deep sense of insecurity among the family, leading Father to consider selling the house. A serious potential buyer even visited to check out the house, but luckily Father changed his mind and did not proceed with the sale. With the population of Jaipur having risen ten-fold to nearly 4 million since the house was constructed, its location now defines more or less the centre of the city. Consequently, the price of the plot has skyrocketed, to somewhere between Rs 100 million and Rs 150 million.

It turned out that after paying the instalment on the house loan, Father's take-home salary was insufficient to meet even the bare essential expenses of the family. Therefore, it was decided to rent half of the house until the loan was fully paid. As originally built, the house had four rooms and another, very small room on the first floor. The family ended up living in two rooms while the remaining two rooms were rented out. We used the small room on the first floor as our study. On the few occasions that Kaka Saheb would stay with us for his treatment, he would end up sleeping in that small room at night. For a family of six this was a tight squeeze, but with enough open spaces in the house in the form of a veranda next to the rooms, an adjacent large walled yard, a veranda outside at the entrance to the house, a lawn in the front yard, and a big backyard where we planted various fruit trees and even carved out our own little plots to grow peanuts, it did not feel that way.

After the house loan was paid, Father was able to take loans for house repairs and a car. Rather than spend the funds on repairs to the main house, he invested them in adding a room to the main building and creating an annexe in a small part of the empty space in the backyard. We, the three brothers, got the new room in the main building as our study. Kamala got the small room on the first floor that had served as the study for all of us till then. As for the annexe at the back, Father rented it to a family and used the proceeds to pay the instalments on the house-repair and car loans.

By the time Father retired in June 1976, all loans had been fully repaid and he had no liabilities left. In the years following his retirement, he only added assets and incurred no liabilities. As such, when he passed away, we only inherited assets. Well before passing away, he also made a clear will delineating how the house should be divided among his children, should they decide to do so. He also willed that Kamala should have the use of the annexe in the back, should she choose to live there. That eliminated a common source of friction among siblings after their parents pass away. Later, Mother did the same with her jewellery before passing in 2015.

Father's sacrifice of his personal career so that his children may build theirs did not go in vain. Including me, we are five – three brothers and two sisters. The three brothers are all younger than the two sisters. I am the youngest. I did my MA in economics, securing the first rank in the entire University of Rajasthan. I then went on to do a PhD in economics at Princeton University. During the last fifteen years, I have been a professor at Columbia University in the United States. From January 2015 to August 2017, I served as the first vice chairman of the NITI Aayog, with the rank of a cabinet minister. The NITI Aayog is the think tank

Prime Minister Narendra Modi created as a successor institution to the erstwhile Planning Commission. In 2012, the government of India honoured me with the Padma Bhushan.

Moving from the youngest to the older siblings, Ashok comes next. He went on to join the medical profession. After spectacular performances in both MBBS and MD at SMS Medical College in Jaipur, he became the first medical professional from Rajasthan to become a Doctor of Medicine or DM in neurology. In 2002, the Medical Council of India awarded him the Dr B.C. Roy medal, the highest Indian award in the medical field. The government of India topped that by honouring him with a Padma Shri in 2014. As a physician, he is a legend in India and has contributed to saving thousands of lives during his long and illustrious career as a neurologist.

My eldest brother Ravi was the brightest of us all, ranking twenty-fourth among tens of thousands of students taking the high-school board examination and ninth university-wide in his first-year BSc examination. He appropriately went into engineering, the most competitive and coveted field of his time (the medical profession was seen as a fallback option for those who could not make it to engineering in those days). He distinguished himself as a student of metallurgical engineering at what is now known as the Malviya National Institute of Technology. The institute appointed him as an assistant professor immediately after his graduation. He later joined the private sector and went on to serve as the senior vice president of Hindustan Electro Graphite Ltd. The Institute of Engineers, India, has honoured him twice with the 'Outstanding Engineer' award.

My sister Kamala is next. Like me, she chose to go into the arts faculty and did an MA in political science in the mid 1960s.

The traditional course for young women in those days was to get married after completing their bachelor's or master's degree. With my eldest sister Premlata already married in the late 1950s, that was also the wish of both my parents for Kamala. But Kamala was the most strongheaded of us all and chose to defy tradition. She remained single for life. After her MA, she did a BEd degree and went on to distinguish herself as a teacher, retiring as the principal of a senior higher secondary school in Jaipur. For her services as a teacher, she received a state award in 1992 and a presidential award in 1995.

Though Father did not live to see Ashok and I receive our Padma awards, his interventions in our early lives were critical to these and other of our achievements. He expected us to work hard, especially at our studies, and saw to it that we did. He moulded our thinking and careers, even risking the possibility that in the event of failure we might grow up to resent him for pushing us into careers we did not choose.

By the time Ravi was in the eighth grade, Ashok in the sixth and I in the fourth, Father had come to a decision on what our career paths would be. By this time, Ravi's talent in mathematics and science was clearly evident. In those days, most bright students went into engineering, which offered an assured decent job. But Father felt that Ravi was too bright for engineering and should aspire to be a scientist. Accordingly, he had him opt for science and mathematics for his high school diploma. Father's plan was that Ravi would do an MSc in physics or some other branch of science. But after the first year of his BSc, Ravi decided that he would rather be an engineer and switched courses.

Father was also of the view that there should be a doctor in the family, and no one had a better personality and temperament for it than Ashok. Therefore, from the time Ashok was in the sixth grade, Father began motivating him towards a career in medical science. Mahaveer School, where we brothers began our schooling, did not offer biology in high school. Therefore, after Ashok completed his eighth grade, he transferred to a school that offered biology, which was a required subject of study in secondary school for those wishing to enter a medical college. Ashok became a doctor, as planned for by Father, and eventually specialized in neurology.

My case was probably the most complicated of the three brothers. Having himself been in administration and perhaps appreciative of the value of public service, Father wanted one of us to go into administration, and specifically, join the IAS. By the process of elimination, I was the automatic choice for this, but there was more to matching me with administration than it being the default choice for me. My father thought that I had both the talent and the right bent of mind to succeed in administration. In those days, I was certainly the most argumentative of all the family members.

Father had figured that given the structure of the IAS written examinations and the skills I would need as an officer, the best course for me would be to study history, economics and mathematics for my BA, and economics for my MA. History, economics and mathematics would provide me ample flexibility to select my papers for the written IAS examinations, while more advanced training in economics would come in handy for me as an officer. To have recognized the importance of economics in the early 1960s, when few appreciated its value in a place like Jaipur, testifies to his connect with the outside world.

For my tenth-grade diploma, Father thought it was fine for me to study science and mathematics. That was my choice too.

Therefore, I continued in Mahaveer School after the eighth grade. During these years, he kept motivating me to switch to arts after the tenth grade, though not wholly successfully. I did quite well in my tenth-grade board examinations, ranking among the top 1 per cent of those taking the board examination and scoring distinction in mathematics and chemistry. In those days, anyone studying arts or commerce was automatically assumed to be inferior to those studying science and mathematics. Acutely aware of this stigma, and having done well in my tenth-grade examinations, I had remained reluctant to switching to arts. But I was pliable, and Father prevailed.

I had always believed that Father had no qualms about giving me the necessary push for the switch. Only recently did I learn from Ravi that, on the contrary, Father remained anxious the whole of the following year on account of it. He feared that if I ended up doing poorly in arts I would blame him for my failure the rest of my life. It was only the day the results of my pre-university examinations came out and I scored the top rank in the entire university that he breathed easy. That was the day Father told Ravi that he had been worried all year that if I did not do well I might blame him for my failure.

In the end, I did not follow the path Father had chosen for me to its final destination of IAS. Nevertheless, I did substantively fulfil the mission he had chosen for me. After a long academic career in the United States, in January 2015, I returned to India for three years to work at the NITI Aayog in the central government at the highest level and fulfil the mission of public service my father had envisaged for me. Given the importance of the position I held, I was perhaps able, in those three years, to contribute more to public causes than I might have via a lifetime career as an IAS officer. Moreover, my writings as an academic during the past twenty years have focused directly on public policy in India, which too is a form of public service.

Regarding my sister, Kamala, as stated, Father had the traditional view that after her bachelor's degree she should be married. As such, he did not charter any specific career path for her. But Kamala thought differently and went on to become the principal of a senior higher secondary school.

Father was friendly towards us but also commanded our unqualified respect. That was essential if he was going to be able to enforce the discipline that he saw as necessary for our success. By the late 1960s, a new room had been added to the house, which we three brothers shared as our study room. Ravi and Ashok also slept in that room, while I slept in the common family room. Each evening, Father would make at least one random visit to our room to check that we were studying and not goofing off. If he caught us dozing or wasting our time chatting, a scolding would invariably follow. More often than not, one of us would hear his approaching footsteps in the direction of our room and quickly alert the others.

Father also insisted that we went to bed by 10 p.m. He wanted us to rise early in the morning. He was regular with his early morning walks with his friends and would come to our room to wake us up before heading out. Sometimes, his friends would arrive early to fetch him and he would miss the chance to wake us up. On those days, we would manage to steal a few extra minutes of sleep.

We three brothers studied at Shree Mahaveer Digambar Jain High School (later converted into a senior higher secondary school) till tenth grade, except Ashok, who switched to Podar

School after his eighth grade. The school charged a minimal fee – just four rupees per month, according to my memory. It was a short walk from our rented house on M.I. Road, where we lived till 1957. Our second rented house in C-Scheme area was just as close to our school. But in 1959, we moved to the house that Father had got built. The distance between this house and the school was a solid 2.5 kilometres. At the time, we brothers were just seven, nine and eleven years old. We all thought this was a punishingly long distance to walk each way.

Given its limited space, Mahaveer School used to run two shifts, a morning shift for grades one to eight, and an afternoon shift for grades nine and ten. This meant that till we got into the ninth grade, we had to be at school by 7.30 a.m. in the winters and by 7.00 a.m. the rest of the year. Getting up early enough to arrive on time, especially during winters, was a real challenge. But Father had no ear for our complaints. Having himself walked between Suwana and Banera many times at our age, and between Jain Hostel and Maharana College in Udaipur later, he thought the walk was good for our health and mental discipline. At times, Mother's heart would melt and she would spare us some change from the household budget to take a rickshaw for the second half of the way when returning home. But many times, even rickshaws would not be available or would demand half a rupee in fare instead of the quarter rupee we were willing to pay.

During summer breaks, Father would encourage us to join him on his morning walks. Though we joined him sometimes, we were generally reluctant participants, arguing that the summer vacation was our only opportunity to get some leisurely sleep. He also encouraged us to do daily exercise and taught us some yoga asanas. I could never get the hang of shirshasana, though I did manage to learn some of the other important asanas. I found it difficult to maintain regularity in my practice then, but have rediscovered the exercises more recently. For the past decade, I have been spending eight to ten minutes on some simple yoga exercises each morning, which has proved highly beneficial. I have also begun to go for walks, measuring up to five kilometres a day on average.

Our education was supremely important to Father and he closely monitored our progress. At school, I used to have monthly tests, a half-yearly examination and a final examination. I remember that after each examination, even the monthly tests, upon returning from office, Father would ask how I had done in the examination and then go over every single question in the examination paper. He would inspire me to be the best student in the class. He would often say that you should be the best at what you do. If you are going to be Sherpa, be Tenzing. I met his expectations sometimes, but not always. Every now and then a particularly bright student would transfer into my class and edge me out.

He remained focused on education even when it came to the grandchildren. Whenever he would speak to Amita, either during our visits to Jaipur or on the phone to her in the United States, his first question would invariably be about whether the children were doing well in their studies. Ravi was subject to the same enquiries about his daughters, Meghana and Nidhi, when he visited Jaipur, while Ashok's two daughters, Aditi and Arushi, and son Arihant, who lived in the same family house, were subject to direct scrutiny.

Father was a voracious reader. I recall there always being one or two thick books on the central table in his room. These were mostly books on contemporary politics or political history relating to India or the world. He had no interest in fiction and I never saw him read a book that fell in this category. Every couple of months, new books would replace the old ones on his table. A few of the titles that stick in my memory from the 1960s and early 1970s are *The Untold Story* by B.M. Kaul, *The Himalayan Blunder* by J.P. Dalvi, *Integration of Indian States* by V. P. Menon, *India: The Critical Years* by Kuldip Nayar and *The New Industrial Estate* by J.K. Galbraith. Since few in the Rajasthan secretariat were in the habit of reading, he had no difficulty checking out the books from its library and keeping them as long as it took him to read them.

Since his school days, Father had developed a deep interest in the lives of eminent leaders. As a result, he had read biographies or autobiographies of such major figures from around the world as Mahatma Gandhi, Pandit Nehru, Winston Churchill, Charles de Gaulle, Field Marshal Montgomery, Bertrand Russell, Albert Einstein, Rabindranath Tagore, Lord Mountbatten, Charles Chaplin, John F. Kennedy and many others who had inspired generations of young men and women. In the course of writing his own books on the history of Rajasthan later in his life, he read nearly all the major works available on the subject. And he did much original research when writing his books on the freedom movement and on state politics in Rajasthan.

Besides his love of books, there was his passion for bridge. For four decades preceding the last five years of his life, he had a group of bridge players who would gather to play the game every Sunday. Each would play host by rotation for the game. When our house was the venue, Mother would have to make tea and snacks many times, and one of us brothers would serve them. Frequently, my father would get upset with his bridge partner when he made a mistake that led to their losing a game. We would hear him yell, 'Partner, what did you do? You just don't know how to play.' Or, 'Partner, when will you learn to play?' There were one or two players who were not as good as others at the game, and they got called to join only when the group was one or two persons short. Father would send one of us brothers to go and fetch them. One of them would often complain to us on the way that he was treated like a spare tyre, called to join in only when one of the regulars was unavailable. The stakes in the game were small, being no more than five to ten rupees exchanging hands in any one sitting.

The game lasted several hours, but on many occasions it would go on into the early hours of the next morning. If this happened when someone other than Father was hosting the game, Mother would get more and more anxious as the night advanced. By 1 or 2 a.m., she would lose patience and wake up Ravi – that was the curse of being the oldest son – and tell him to find out whether Father might have had an accident while returning home.

Until 1967, when Father became deputy secretary, we had no phone. But even after we got the phone, most other members of Father's bridge team did not. Therefore, Ravi had no option but to go in person to the house of person hosting the game to verify that Father was well. Since the bicycle was the only vehicle the family had until the late 1960s, the two-way trip often took forty minutes to an hour in the dead of night. But Ravi had the coolest head among all the siblings and he carried the burden with good cheer.

The following morning, when Father returned, Mother would be very upset with him, sometimes declaring herself on fast for an indefinite period. It would take a day or two, sometimes longer, for normal communication between her and Father to resume. But the situation would hardly change, with the cycle repeating itself in another few weeks. We all knew that Father could not live without bridge and Mother could not help getting anxious whenever he stayed out till late playing the game. The two of them and the rest of us had to live with those facts.

Father had abiding faith in God. He passed on the family tradition of faith in the deity Hanuman, especially Balaji of Sindri, to the next generation. I recall that he had memorized the Hanuman aarti and once wrote it for us on a piece of paper. He also led the Lakshmi pooja every Diwali evening. There was a long period of time when the entire family, including he, fasted on Tuesdays, eating only one meal that day. He was not averse to visiting temples, but I saw him do that only rarely. He positively disliked religious dogma. I cannot recall a single instance of a pandit coming to our house to perform any rituals.

Among religious books, Father's two favourites were the *Bhagavad Geeta* and *Uttaradhyayan Sutra*. The former synthesizes the competing strands of Hindu thought while the latter is the most important sacred book of Shvetambar Jains (our family is Shvetambar Jain), believed to contain the actual words of Mahavir, the founder of Jainism. His collection of books included the English translation of the *Bhagavad Gita* by S. Radhakrishnan, *Satyarth Prakash* by Swami Dayananda Saraswati and several volumes on Swami Vivekananda.

At a practical level, Father had great respect for all religions. I remember how, after we had moved to our new house in 1959, one by one, he collected nice big posters of the founders of all the major religions, got them framed and hung them in our family room. There were pictures of the Buddha, Mahavir, Christ and Guru Nanak. In 1975, on the occasion of the 2500th anniversary of the nirvana of Lord Mahavir, Father helped found a cultural, philanthropic and social service organization called Mahavir

International. Today, this is a vast organization with more than 125 branches around the world.

While framing the constitution of Mahavir International, Father successfully inserted in it the provision that this will be a society meant to serve the destitute, irrespective of their caste, creed or religion, and that any person belonging to any faith would be welcome to become its member and office bearer as long as she subscribed to the broad principles of 'Live and Let Live' and 'Love All Serve All', as enunciated by Mahavir. I remember assisting Father in the work of the organization when I came for my first visit back home from the United States in the summer of 1976. The earliest activity of the organization had consisted of issuing a small number of scholarships to bright but needy students. I remember reviewing the applications and helping Father with the final selection.

Given that he was an active participant in the freedom movement, it is no surprise that Father was very nationalistic. He also did his best to pass on that sense of nationalism to his children. One of the things he did towards this end was to seek out portraits of all the leaders he admired, frame them and hang them up in his drawing room. Upon entering his room, the first thing anyone noticed were majestic portraits of Mahatma Gandhi, Pandit Nehru, Sardar Patel, Rajendra Prasad, S. Radhakrishnan and Indira Gandhi.

Father also named the children in the family after well-known contemporary and historical figures. His sister's son was the first child to be born in the extended family following his generation. He named him Mohan, after Mahatma Gandhi. Ravi, whose full formal name is Ravindra, was named after Rabindranath Tagore. Ashok was named after Emperor Ashoka, and I after

Aurobindo Ghosh. Then, when my eldest son was born, Father named him Hirsh, after the emperor Harsha Vardhan. In India, the name is spelt Harsh, but we tweaked it a little since in the United States the conventional spelling would have been understood to mean 'unpleasant' (harsh), which is almost the opposite of its meaning – happy or joyful – in Hindi. In the hospital, soon after his birth, we had given him the name Ananth. So, his name ended up becoming Ananth Hirsh.

Father was very social and had a large network of friends. He had served in the Government of Rajasthan during a period when institutions and systems were being put in place. As a result, he had had the opportunity to employ many people. In two of his stints, at Malviya Regional Engineering College and at State Insurance, he had directly hired many individuals. As the staff welfare officer in the secretariat, he also solved the pension and seniority issues of numerous employees. Many of those employees remained loyal to him and would occasionally come by to see him even after his retirement. With his network of friends, he also helped friends or friends of friends to clear bureaucratic hurdles in various sections of the state government. This further expanded his network of friends.

An important reason for his large network was his friendly personality. He had an uncanny ability to relate to people of any age. As result, many of my own and my brothers' friends became his 'friends' too. He would often be sitting in the front lawn in the evening, reading the newspaper or a book, and one of our friends would show up. He would ask him to come and sit next to him and immediately draw him into conversation. Over time, many of our friends had also grown very fond of Father. Though I had left India in 1974, some of my friends continued to visit our house to see him. One of them eventually ended up co-authoring a book with him. Ashok also had a large network of friends, and Father indulged them regularly. Later, Ashok inherited Father's networking skills. I recall even Father being very impressed with the network of friends and acquaintances Ashok had created.

Father had a great connect with children also. On one of our visits in the late 1980s, Amita had taken the children on a visit to the local zoo in Jaipur. Ajay must have been less than five years old then. Father was sitting in the lawn when they returned from the zoo. So he immediately called them over to sit with him and started chatting with young Ajay. He asked him, 'Did you see the "beer" (bear) at the zoo?' Ajay replied, 'You mean bear?' Father said, 'Yes, beer, did you see it?' Ajay said, 'You are saying "beer", which is a drink that makes you dizzy. "Bear" is an animal.' Like many Indians, Father was pronouncing 'bear' as 'beer', and Ajay was quick to point out the flaw in his pronunciation. This was a bit of turning of tables, since during our days as children, Father would never miss the opportunity to correct our English pronunciation, learned from teachers in our Hindi-medium school. But at that point, Father quickly turned to an interrogation of Amita, asking her, 'How come Ajay knows about beer at such a young age?' So Amita had to explain why Ajay knew about this drink!

So far, the gene for sports has been missing in our family. Other than Ajay, who has done some serious trekking, mountain climbing and rowing, none of us has been a serious participant in any outdoor activity, let alone competitive sports. Father played some recreational cricket while at Maharana College in Udaipur, as did we during our school days. We also played the game at home, either in the driveway or on the road outside, which was almost free of traffic during the 1960s. Both the field and equipment were improvised. The field was narrow, allowing the batsman to hit the ball only straight ahead. The equipment consisted of a tennis ball, a used bat and the 'mudda' (a traditional relaxation seat made of straw for use in the garden) with its backrest as the wicket. On rare occasions, Father would join us.

Though not a sportsperson, Father did have a passion for watching cricket, especially Test matches. Till 1974, when I left India, there was no television in Jaipur. The principal medium for following the matches closely was the running commentary broadcast on All India Radio. Those were the days of commentators such as Vijay Merchant, Devraj Puri, Anand Setalvad, Vizzy (Maharajkumar Vizianagram), Berry Sarbadhikari and Dicky Rutnagur. After we got a telephone in the house, if a test match was being played, Father would call a few times during the day from his office to find out the score. Sometimes he would want to listen to the running commentary for a few minutes to an hour. At those times, I would hold the phone receiver close to the radio while the commentary played. If the game was lacking action or if a particularly bad commentator came to replace a better one, he would hang up. But if the game was going well, he would stay on the line for almost an hour. By the time he retired, television had arrived and he could watch the games live. That greatly added to the value of his leisure time during retirement.

Father maintained a very simple life. After his retirement, with all the children becoming independent and even able to contribute to family expenses, the financial condition of the family considerably improved. But it was impossible to persuade him to treat himself to any comforts, let alone luxuries. An air cooler had been installed in his room by the late 1970s, but he would hardly use it because it made too much noise. On my visits to India, I would ask him if he would like me to bring him anything from the United States. But his only demand was shaving blades. After I took him a shaving kit, including a razor, from the United States in 1981, he discovered how bad the locally manufactured blades were. After that, till India's liberalization finally brought the same razor and blades to retail shops in Jaipur, his standard question upon my arrival in Jaipur would be, 'Did you bring the blades?' The only other product I remember taking for him from the United States was playing cards. Once again, the quality of even the relatively inexpensive cards I would bring was far superior to what he could get locally. The cards I would bring also lasted long, so that I did not have to bring them at the same frequency as the shaving blades.

Outwardly, Father maintained his composure, and for the most part his outer appearance did not give away his emotions. But during the times he had to part from any of the family members, you could see him choke. The first time I noticed it was when Ravi left home to take up a job in Jodhpur. When I left home for the United States in 1974, he came up to Delhi along with Ashok to see me off. That parting was evidently tough on him. Then, when Ashok left to study for his DM degree at the Post Graduate Institute in Chandigarh in 1981, Father had a serious anxiety attack since he had always stayed at home until then. That was the time Amita and I had just got married and we happened to be home. I recall that we had to call a doctor, deputed by Ashok, that evening. The doctor gave Father a tranquilizer and tried to calm us down with the assurance that once he'd had a good sleep overnight, he would be fine. We found out the following morning that the doctor was right.

Parting after a visit home became progressively more painful for us as Father advanced in age. The cheer on his face would be gone and he would tell Amita, 'So you are leaving. Remember to inform of your safe arrival immediately upon reaching home. Take good care of the children.' As the years passed, the common fear at parting on both sides was whether this would be the last time we would get to see each other. By the grace of God, Father got to live many more years than most in his generation and we got lots of opportunities to return home to see him and be with him.

Father generally maintained good health. His weight remained more or less constant, at around fifty kilograms during the last forty-five years of his life. Consistent with this weight, he ate small meals and kept a good balance of nutrients in his diet. He also remained regular in his morning walks. These factors kept him generally healthy, but not without episodes of serious illness. Between the late 1980s and 2001, there were three occasions when the family feared they might lose him, but thanks to the magical medical powers of Ashok, he was successfully treated each time. It was fortuitous that of the three sons, the only one who stayed in Jaipur was Ashok, the doctor.

The first episode was a relatively minor one. Father had returned home after visiting a friend. Since the entrance door was closed from inside, he rang the bell. In all probability, his blood pressure dropped and he felt dizzy. He dropped down onto one of the muddas that usually stayed in the outside verandah. When the door was opened, he was found lying unconscious on the mudda. Ashok was immediately called. He gave him the necessary emergency treatment and took my father to the hospital. Father recovered quickly. So as not to worry me, Ashok did not inform me about the episode, and I learned about it only on my next visit to Jaipur.

The second episode occurred in early 1993 and involved a mild heart attack. It was definitely more serious and Ashok called me on the phone right away, directing me to be ready to leave for Jaipur on short notice in case my father's condition deteriorated. I was working at the World Bank at the time and alerted my division that I may have to leave for India on just a few hours' notice. Father was admitted to a local hospital that specialized in cardiology. He got good care and gradually recovered. Once he seemed out of danger, Ashok advised that rather than come and leave in a hurry, I might as well come later when I could spend some time with Father.

It was the third episode that proved to be most serious. This was in March 2001. Father was already eighty years old, so any illness could pose a threat to his life. This time, when Ashok called me, he was not circumspect and I left immediately for Jaipur. I arrived on 17 March 2001 and found my father to be seriously ill. Ashok felt that since treatment for the illness involved no surgery and he could arrange all medical care at home, it was better not to admit him in the hospital. The family were very tense, fearing that we might lose him this time around.

In the following week, I witnessed two inexplicable events that are worth narrating. These are events of the kind that everyone experiences from time to time in their lives and have no rational explanation for them. Therefore, we call them coincidences. The first one is about a parallel between the ups and downs in my father's illness and those in India's fortunes in the cliffhanger third cricket test match of the Border-Gavaskar trophy series played in Chennai between 18 and 22 March 2001. This was the final test match in a three-match series between India and Australia. With Australia having won the first match played in Mumbai and India the second one played in Kolkata, this third match was to decide the series winner.

The match was full of twists and turns of fortunes. It began with Australia winning the toss the third time in a row and electing to bat. By the end of the first day, 18 March, they had racked up a formidable score of 326 runs with only three wickets lost. The second day, India finally got a break. Early in the morning, a ball from Harbhajan Singh hit the left pad of Australian captain Steve Waugh and then swung back towards the stumps. Waugh instinctively put his glove in the way of the ball, diverting it away from the wicket. Upon appeal, he was declared out, becoming only the sixth player ever in test cricket to lose his wicket for touching the ball. After that, Harbhajan Singh bundled out the remaining six Australian players for just twenty-six runs. Nevertheless, with the total score of Australia at 391 runs, the odds were against India.

It turned out, however, that when India came to bat, it played one of its best innings. It ended the second day with 211 runs for just one wicket. The Indian batsmen held the wicket the entire third day, reaching 480 runs for nine wickets. They ended the innings at 501 runs the fourth day. It appeared that India was all set to win the game.

The Australian team returned to bat. Expectedly, with the pitch having turned softer on the fourth day, they could not go far and ended the fourth day with 241 for seven wickets. On the fifth day, the remaining three wickets fell in quick succession, with the innings ending at a total score of 264. Once again, Harbhajan

Singh bagged eight wickets. With only 155 runs to score, victory looked well within India's grasp.

But the Indian team had a quick collapse in the fourth innings. By lunch, they had lost the first wicket with the score at just twenty-three. By tea, they were 132 for five wickets. After tea, they lost another two wickets for just two more runs. To win, India still needed twenty-one runs and had only tailenders left. Harbhajan Singh came after the fall of the seventh wicket. He once again proved India's saviour, giving stand to wicketkeeper S.S. Dighe at the other end. Dighe added eighteen runs and Harbhajan contributed the remaining three. That decided the game and the series in India's favour.

On 17 March, when I arrived in India, and during the five days of the cricket match, my father's illness exhibited almost an identical pattern. Upon arrival, I had found him in a very fragile state. At fifty kilos, he was never a physically strong person, so that even minor illnesses were sufficient to knock him down. The external symptoms we could all see were fever, extreme weakness and non-stop hiccuping. He was lying in bed throughout. Ashok had diagnosed this to be the result of some infection in the body, most likely in the kidney. Accordingly, he was treating him with antibiotics. For the first four days, his condition showed no improvement. Then, on 21 March, the day India ended its first innings at 501 runs, he showed signs of improvement. Ashok looked sufficiently hopeful and relaxed for me to gather the motivation to even go out to shop for a few things that I needed to bring to the United States.

But on 22 March, Father's condition began deteriorating again. Indeed, it deteriorated to the point that by 8 p.m. Ashok felt that it was time to shift him to the hospital. When he announced this decision, Mother looked at him grimly and asked, 'So there is no hope anymore?' Ashok answered her question with silence. We all began to prepare ourselves mentally for the worst. My ticket for the return flight to the United States was for the night of 24 March. I thought I would need to change my flight. By 9 p.m., Ashok had left with Father for the hospital.

The next day, I got ready early in the morning and made my way to the hospital. As I reached there and arrived in the ward where Father was admitted, I noticed that Ashok had a broad smile on his face. I asked him how it looked and he said with a grin that all was well. Apparently, he had run tests for kidney infection and found them to be negative. That led him to the possibility that the infection was in the lungs instead, which turned out to be the case. The lung infection also explained the persistence of hiccups. Once the problem was pinpointed, targeted antibiotics generated instant response. I asked Ashok if I should nevertheless go ahead and change my travel plans to a later date. He answered unequivocally in the negative.

After India had snatched victory from the jaws of defeat in the match in Chennai on the afternoon of 22 March, I had hoped that my father would pull off a similar miracle. Therefore, it was disappointing when Ashok announced later that day that the opposite had transpired, with his condition deteriorating to the point that it was time to move him to the hospital. Little did I know at the time that the miracle the cricket match had signalled was indeed going to happen and the parallel between the two events I had been following since my arrival would turn out to be complete! On the flight back to the United States, the parallel between the cricket match and Father's illness kept playing in a loop in my mind. I even thought that if I were a literary writer rather than an economist, I could have adapted the entire experience into a good short story.

The second miracle I mentioned concerns an astrological prediction. While I have never made any decision in my life based on such predictions, I have always found it fun to discuss horoscopes with astrologers. Ashok and his son Arihant have great expertise in the subject, and Amita and I have long discussions on the horoscopes of our children with them each time we visit India. I have to say that I know of no rational or scientific basis on which prediction of future events in the life of an individual can be made. Yet I have seen horoscope predictions to come true in more cases and with greater accuracy than you would expect from any other model of prediction. A sceptic would say that predictions fail to come true in the vast majority of cases. While I would agree with this assertion, the surprise is that an inexplicable number of them comes true and with great accuracy.

In the present context, the evening that we lost all hope that Father would recover and Ashok moved him to the hospital, my maternal uncle's son, who had been deeply into consulting astrologers throughout his life, called from Bhilwara. He spoke to Ashok before he left for the hospital. He told Ashok that he had just come from consulting the astrologer who had originally drawn up Father's horoscope. According to this astrologer, nothing untoward was going to happen to Father for the next five years. Given his condition at the time, the prediction seemed nothing more than an effort to console the family in its time of deep sadness. None of us believed it. And yet, it proved true with a remarkable degree of precision. My father not only recovered from this episode of illness but also lived for another four years and nine months.

After the episode in 2001, my father experienced no major illness till the day he passed away. On that fateful day, death was quick and painless. This being said, he did experience a loss of quality of life during the last three or four years of his life. The main factor had been a steady deterioration in his reading vision. He had suffered from mild diabetes, which probably led to gradual macular degeneration. While he could otherwise see and function normally, he could not read. Given that reading and writing had been his entire existence during the many preceding decades, this created a major void in his life.

Amita and I visited him frequently during these years. We would try to visit separately so that the number of visits could be multiplied. We would also call Father on the phone frequently, thanks to the vast technological change that had brought the cost of international calls crashing down. When I first came to the United States in 1974, it had cost me $12 for the three-minute call I made to inform the family that I had safely arrived at Princeton. But now we could call for a few pennies per minute. Father would always ask how the children were progressing and how my own work was coming along. In 2004, I had moved to Columbia in New York from the University of Maryland at College Park on the outskirts of Washington, DC, where he had visited us in 1985. That move made him immensely proud and happy. He had known of my friendship with Professor Jagdish Bhagwati, who too was at Columbia, and he would occasionally ask me how my friend was doing.

During the last year of his life, I had been working on a major book on India, which later came out under the title *India: The*

Emerging Giant in 2008. On our phone calls, he would always ask how the book was progressing. When he asked that question in the last call I had with him, I said, 'It is progressing but will take a little time to complete.' Having authored several books himself, he had a good understanding of how the process of writing works and what a good writer should strive for. So he replied, 'Take your time but write a definitive book on India.' Those were his last words to me.

Though we had moved to New York in October 2004, we had held on to our house in Bethesda, Maryland. On the occasional weekend and during longer breaks, Amita and I used to come back to the house. We did the same during the winter break following the end of the fall 2005 semester. On 31 December 2005, we had invited a few friends to dinner to celebrate New Year's Eve.

One of the guests asked Amita whether she was planning to visit India during the winter break. She emphatically replied, 'Absolutely not. Given the fog in Delhi and the delays in local flights it causes, I would never ever go to India in the month of January.' She had no idea that a call for such a visit was only a few hours away.

The next morning, after I settled in my study chair with tea to begin the day, the phone rang. Amita, who was there in the same room with her cup of tea, said it must be a Happy New Year call. But, alas, the call was the saddest it could be. It was Ashok at the other end, informing us that Father was no more. From my response, Amita understood what had happened and broke into tears immediately. The same happened to me as I got off the phone and turned to begin making flight reservations for the same day. That evening, I left for Jaipur. Amita followed two days later, and sure enough, after she boarded the local flight to Jaipur from Delhi, fog descended and her plane was forced to sit on the tarmac for three hours.

Father had not asked us to commemorate his death with a community feast and we did not do it. Such a feast would have been contrary to everything he had stood for. As per custom, we did hold a formal condolence meeting the third day following his passing away. The stream of guests who came to say their last goodbyes that day was endless. When Father had first come to Jaipur in 1946 to work at the newspaper *Lokvani*, there were hardly any cars to be seen anywhere in the city. And this day, when he left it for good, there were easily one-kilometre-long lines of cars parked on each side of the venue of the meeting. And, of course, many among the guests came on scooters, bicycles and on foot.

At the conclusion of the meeting, we brothers stood for more than an hour at the door as the guests emptied the big meeting hall one by one. Among them, there must have been some who were Father's friends or the children of his friends who were no more, others who had worked with him during his more than fifty years of active life, and still others who had been beneficiaries of his generosity. As we stood bidding goodbye to one and all, one of the guests stopped briefly near Ashok and whispered, 'Doctor Saheb, he was my father too!' Given the good Father had done to so many during his life, there must have been many more in the sea of people who felt the same way.

9

In Retrospect

THIS IS MY FIRST attempt at writing a biography. The process has turned out to be a journey in which I got an introduction to my father that I did not have while he lived. I had read his autobiography even in manuscript form, and then had re-read it after he got it printed. Yet, as a reader, I did not appreciate the importance of the many events in his life, especially those relating to the phase prior to the formation of Rajasthan. It was only in the course of trying to piece together a coherent narrative that I began to see how rich his life had been. That process of discovery also raised many questions in my mind that I would have asked him had I done this while he still lived. What made Grandmother so proud and unbending, and where did her impeccable value system come from? What were his thoughts as he walked from Suwana to Banera the first time? What was his relationship with his mausi and mausa in Banera? What led him to eventually quit wearing khadi and the Gandhi cap? Did he think that he might have had a shot at becoming the chief minister of Rajasthan had he made the same decision as his colleagues Shiv Charan Mathur and N.N. Acharya?

No doubt, some critically inclined readers of the biography will feel that my narrative has been one-sided, focusing only on what was positive in my father's life and carefully screening out what was negative. In this they would be right. To be sure, Father was a normal human, and with some effort I could perhaps draw a list of half a dozen character flaws in him. Yet, I have chosen not to do so for two reasons.

First, those flaws have little to do with the story I wanted bring to the readers – the story of a boy who was born amid no hope whatsoever, went on to join the Indian freedom movement, helped build his state after Independence, championed many public causes as a private citizen and yet remained largely unknown. Inserting his flaws for the sake of a 'balanced' account of his persona would have only subtracted from rather than added to the core of the story.

Second, with the benefit of having seen him only via intermittent visits during the last three decades of his life, and the passage of an additional sixteen years after his passing away, Father's flaws seem too distant to me. When it comes to individuals in our lives whom we loved and cherished and who are no more, the human mind has an uncanny ability to blur out the negatives associated with them while sharpening the positives. Even his most serious flaws are today dwarfed by what was good in him.

Like the story of any person who has lived a noble life, my father's life offers lessons in what makes a good human being and what parents must do to make good citizens out of their children.

I come to some of these lessons in the second half of this chapter. But, somewhat unexpectedly for an economist, my father's life story also provides a window to two important issues of public policy. On both, his life reinforces what good economics tells us.

First and foremost, Father's story brings into sharp relief how powerful a weapon education can be for the betterment of an individual's, and therefore the nation's, life. He and his family had absolutely nothing when he was born, not even the means to scrape together two decent meals a day. My grandmother, who raised him till fourteen years of age, probably had no education herself. Yet, somehow, living as far back as in the 1920s and 1930s in a remote village, she could figure that education might provide my father a path to a decent life. That single insight opened the doors to a rich life, not just for my father and mother but also for those of us who followed. I shudder to think what life would have been for all of us had Grandmother decided against sending her only son to study in Banera at the age of ten. Or if Father had lacked the motivation and courage to leave the safety of his mother's home and undertake that twelve-mile-long walk from Suwana to Banera.

In the light of his own personal experience, it is no surprise then that Father was convinced that the best thing he could do for us, his children, was to impart to us the best education possible. I recall that when a friend of his once asked him if he had any investments, he pointed his finger towards us. But his personal experience could take him only so far. The circumstances of his life and ours were very different. Whereas he could build his life on a high school diploma, later complemented by a law degree, we faced a very different world. We were going to face competition from children who were getting educated at expensive, elite schools. Father lacked the financial resources to send us to those schools. Therefore, he had to fill the gap by paying enormous personal attention to our education at home. That then is another important insight from his experience: accomplishments of children at school depend to a great extent on the attention and supervision parents offer them at home. No amount of coaching can substitute for close supervision at home, especially in the early years of a child's life.

The second policy issue on which my father's life throws light is rural–urban migration. It is an unfortunate aspect of intellectual discourse in India that many well-meaning commentators and policymakers in the country like to glorify the village life and deride rural–urban migration. They argue, with a touch of nostalgia – though most of them lack the credentials for it since they themselves have never lived in a village – that we should create conditions such that farmers would not leave the comfort of rural life for the hard city life, where they would end up living in slums.

I am especially reminded of a thoroughly urbane former rural development minister of India, who once staked the claim that by implementing the National Rural Employment Guarantee Scheme, he had put an end to distress migration out of rural India. Similar sentiments played out in the media when, in the midst of the COVID-19 threat, numerous migrant workers were seen trying to walk hundreds of miles to get back to their homes. Many states, as well as the central government, rushed to allocate billions of rupees' worth of taxpayer money on poorly conceived livelihood programmes that would ensure that these 'poor' migrants would not have to return to the 'hardship' of their city jobs.

In my humble judgement, such thinking is wholly anti-development. Rural–urban migration ought to be encouraged and facilitated rather than shunned and resisted. It is thanks to my father, who migrated from his village against all odds to Jaipur, that in the next generation I could migrate to the United States, get world-class education at Princeton University and then become a professor at Columbia University in New York City. His migration enabled Ashok to become an eminent neurologist, Ravi to get the coveted engineering degree in the 1960s and Kamala to win a presidential award for her services as a teacher. Who can dispute that, by any reasonable metric, my siblings and I have had much richer and prosperous lives than the children of my father's cousin Kanakmal who remained in Suwana?

In the broader context of economic policy, the question we must ask is, why is it that after seventy years of effort to make farmers prosperous, farmer distress remains such a regular feature of our lives? The answer is not hard to see. In every country, including the rich ones such as the United States, farmer distress is a result of droughts, floods and frost. But in countries in which farmers constitute a tiny proportion of the workforce, the remaining workforce can contribute enough financial resources to alleviate the distress. When more than 40 per cent of the workforce is in farming, as in India, and taxpayers comprise a tiny proportion of the population, available revenue resources are meagre and those in distress numerous. Each time we have an episode of farmer distress, we come up with a new scheme, but when calculated on a per-capita basis, the total sum of assistance of all the schemes remains tiny.

What makes the situation of farmers in India worse still in comparison to their counterparts in richer countries is that even when there is no drought or flood, farm incomes do not rise significantly above subsistence level, except for a tiny minority of farmers with large farms. In India, on an average, the value added per worker in agriculture is less than one-fourth of that in industry and services. Given that the latter itself is hardly enough to yield a comfortable living standard, the average value added in farming can give, at best, a subsistence level of existence.

But when it comes to the smaller farmers, the situation is dire. As per the agricultural census of 2015–16, 48 per cent of landholdings in India are smaller than half a hectare, with their average size being just 0.23 hectare.[22] Such tiny holdings can scarcely yield enough to feed a family of five. For these farmers, even the doubling of farm income – by no means an easy task – cannot go far, given its low initial level.

The bottom line is that we cannot bring prosperity to farmers in general and to those working the tiny plots of land in particular without moving half or more of the farm population out of agriculture. It is only by recognizing this fact that we can reorient our policies towards creating well-paid jobs for the unskilled in industry and services and making cities more hospitable for migrating workers.

Under the current policies, the bulk of investible capital gets concentrated in highly capital- or skilled-labour-intensive sectors that create, at best, limited well-paid jobs for the unskilled. Tax revenues collected from these sectors are hardly enough to run social programmes at a level that would give a comfortable existence to the large rural population. Bringing prosperity to the latter requires policies that channel investible resources into employment-intensive industries such as food processing, apparel,

---

22 Calculated from Table 14 in 'Agricultural Census 2015-16', *All India Report on Number and Area of Operational Holdings*, Ministry of Agriculture and Farmers Welfare, Government of India, 2019, pp. 54-55.

footwear, furniture and numerous other light industries that would facilitate rather than impede rural–urban migration.

In parallel, urban housing policy also needs to be reoriented to shift focus from owner-occupied to low-rent dormitory housing for migrant workers. Urban housing schemes in India have focused almost entirely on subsidizing owner-occupied dwellings. Hardly any resources have been devoted to the creation of affordable rental housing. Policies that keep the price of urban land excessively high make the emergence of low-rent commercial housing nearly impossible as well. The result has been that whatever limited rural–urban migration has taken place has led to the creation of slums in the major Indian cities. Poor living conditions in the slums in turn have fed the anti-rural–urban migration sentiment among policy analysts and policy makers alike. Breaking this vicious circle, first and foremost, requires recognition that rural–urban migration is a positive, not negative, force.

Turning to lessons for one's personal life, let me mention four. First, while luck matters occasionally in life, it is hard work, persistence and focus that determine the overall outcomes in life. When events do not go our way, we lose heart and go on to generalize one episode of bad luck into a cursed life. Yet, every individual experiences both good and bad luck throughout their life; it is just that we have a tendency to note bad luck more than we notice good luck. There were times when, at crucial moments, Father's situation looked grim. But before any damage could happen, he had the good luck to come out of those situations. For instance, he had no means to finance his studies in high school in Udaipur, but with effort and some luck he was able to mobilize resources to cover the hostel fee, tuition fee and personal expenses. His situation looked entirely hopeless when the time came to fill in his examination form for high school with a fee of Rs 25, and yet a solution emerged at the very last minute. These were cases of luck eventually coming to his rescue. But he also had times when luck did not help him. When in the Rajasthan government, he was not awarded the seniority he deserved. And subsequently too, he was denied the promotions that should have been rightfully his. But then, he managed to reinvent himself in retirement, in ways that few individuals are able to do. The trick in life is to recognize that luck favours you sometimes but not all the time. Therefore, there is no reason to freeze into inaction; instead, the right thing is to do one's karma and be ready to take advantage of the situation when luck turns favourable.

The second lesson from Father's life is about humility. No matter how much we would like to claim to be self-made, each of us reaps the benefit of the hard work and sacrifice of the previous generations. One could argue that my father was as close to a self-made person as anyone could be. Yet, it is hard to contest, as I am sure my father himself would agree, that without the foresight and sacrifice of his mother, he would have been nothing. It was her recognition that education was the key to securing the future of her son, followed by not just a major financial and emotional sacrifice but also sacrifice of her health and eventually her life, that allowed my father to live a rich and prosperous life.

Today, my siblings and I may boast all we like about our dedication and hard work, but it will always remain true that without Father having first undertaken the journey that brought him from Suwana to Jaipur, and then having sacrificed his own career so that we could get a decent education, none of our achievements would have come to pass. I could come from Jaipur to New York because my father had the courage to leave Suwana and eventually arrive in Jaipur. Indeed, given the difference between his starting point and mine, his accomplishments represent a far greater leap than mine. A family friend once rightly remarked to Ravi, 'Even if you add up the accomplishments of all five of you brothers and sisters, they will fall short of what your father achieved by himself.'

The third lesson is about courage of conviction. A person genuinely interested in upholding the public interest can succeed in his endeavour only if he has courage. Time and again in his life, Father was faced with the choice of doing what he considered to be right and looking the other way and safeguarding his own narrow selfish interests. Each time, he embraced the former course without a second thought. Whether it was the case of standing against the influential doctor who had spent funds allocated for X-ray machines on the purchase of vehicles, or that of challenging his minister on the matter of giving possession of 200 acres' worth of public land to a private individual, or that of taking issue with successive chairmen of Finance Commissions to safeguard the interests of his state, or that of taking on the mighty academics on the issue of Maharana Pratap, Father did what he thought was right without worrying about the consequences for himself.

The fourth and final lesson flowing from the biography is about nurturing attributes such as honesty, humility, self-respect and courage. David Brooks, a *New York Times* columnist, makes the interesting distinction between résumé virtues and eulogy virtues. The former are skills that lead to success in one's profession. The latter are virtues talked about at funerals, such as whether the person was humble, courageous and honest. Résumé virtues can be learned in school, college and the workplace. But eulogy virtues have to be largely nurtured in the family. Parents have to lead their children by example. The refusal by my grandmother, even under the most dire circumstances, to bow to the community panchas after they had insulted her by refusing to participate in my father's wedding party, was a lesson for my father in both self-respect and courage. The promise she took from him from her deathbed to remain honest all his life was her way of hardwiring him for this key virtue. My father carried those values with him and passed them on to us, his children. The result is that all of us siblings have remained honest in our lives, value self-respect, and carry our father's courage of conviction. And so far, our children have adhered to those values too. None of us has become a billionaire, but each of us goes to bed each day with the satisfaction that we have lived our lives without compromising on the values we inherited.

Index

About the Author

Arvind Panagariya is Professor of Economics and Jagdish N. Bhagwati Professor of Indian Political Economy in the School of International and Public Affairs at Columbia University. He is also the Director of the Deepak and Neera Raj Center on Indian Economic Policies at Columbia. He served as the first vice chairman of NITI Aayog from January 2015 to August 2017. He holds a PhD in economics from Princeton University. He is the author of twenty books, among them *India Unlimited: Reclaiming the Lost Glory*. The Government of India honoured Dr Panagariya with the Padma Bhushan in 2012.

